Praise for
a.k.a. "Lost"

"Jim Henderson is a voice for normalized evangelism—heretofore an oxymoron. Henderson has given value back to each Christian's ordinary attempts to simply shine the light of Christ in our everyday encounters, encouraging us to act in faithfulness and put the results in God's hands."

—LYNNE MARIAN, executive editor of *Outreach* magazine

"I can think of no other book that rings as true with what is really happening in the post-Christian generations. Jim Henderson writes from the vantage point of being among the 'lost,' the very people most Christians have distanced themselves from and don't understand. Get several copies of *a.k.a. 'Lost'* and share them with people in your church."

—DAN KIMBALL, pastor and author of *The Emerging Church* and *Emerging Worship*

"If you have a heart for extending the kingdom of God, this book will both challenge and encourage you to make a difference on planet Earth for eternity. And it will take your thinking and turn it on its ear."

—STEVE SJOGREN, conference speaker and author of *Conspiracy of Kindness*

"Jim Henderson has said it well: Ordinary attempts are never ordinary when they are done in the name of Jesus Christ. This truly is a movement that will result in extraordinary results as God uses us in our everyday lives to bring home the people he misses most."

—DR. DAVID FOSTER, senior pastor of Bellevue
Community Church, Nashville, Tennessee,
and author of *Accept No Mediocre Life*

"By reading *a.k.a. 'Lost,'* perhaps you'll become the answer to somebody's first fledgling prayers: 'God, please help me find someone to talk to about my questions and doubt.'"

—BRIAN MCLAREN, pastor and author of *A New Kind
of Christian* and *The Church on the Other Side*

"Jim Henderson hopes to help Christians become the kindest people on earth. Those who read this delightful, honest, and funny book will be taking a good first step. Those who take its wisdom to heart might just get there."

—CHRISTINE WICKER, award-winning journalist
and author of *God Knows My Heart: Finding a
Faith That Fits*

"In his journey into real conversations with real people, Jim Henderson has come to some fascinating and useful conclusions. Check out *a.k.a. 'Lost'* to join the journey and get some great, down-to-earth, practical advice."

—TODD HUNTER, national director of Alpha USA
and former national director of Vineyard USA

a.k.a. "LOST"

DISCOVERING WAYS TO CONNECT WITH THE PEOPLE JESUS MISSES MOST

BY JIM HENDERSON

Foreword by Brian McLaren

WATERBROOK
PRESS

A.K.A. "LOST"
PUBLISHED BY WATERBROOK PRESS
12265 Oracle Boulevard, Suite 200
Colorado Springs, Colorado 80921
A division of Random House, Inc.

All Scripture quotations, unless otherwise indicated, are taken from the *Holy Bible, New International Version®*. NIV®. Copyright © 1973, 1978, 1984 by International Bible Society. Used by permission of Zondervan Publishing House. All rights reserved.

Italics in Scripture quotations reflect the author's added emphasis.

10 Digit ISBN 1-57856-914-1
13 Digit ISBN 978-1-57856-914-4

Library of Congress Cataloging-in-Publication Data
Henderson, Jim, 1947–
    A.k.a. "lost" : discovering ways to connect with the people Jesus misses most / Jim Henderson.—1st ed.
        p. cm.
    Includes bibliographical references.
    ISBN 1-57856-914-1
    1. Witness bearing (Christianity). I. Title: Also known as "lost." II. Title.
BV4520.H45 2005
248'.5—dc22
                                                            2004030272

Printed in the United States of America
2006

10 9 8 7 6 5 4 3 2

This book is dedicated to Barbara—my wife, my mentor, and the love of my life.

CONTENTS

FOREWORD

Today I was interviewed on a Christian talk-radio program. The interview was supposed to focus on my book *A Generous Orthodoxy*. It was clear from somewhere halfway through the second sentence (right after "Today on our show we have noted author and pastor Brian D. McLaren...") that the talk-show host didn't like the word *generous* in the title of my book. He was suspicious about it, as if being generous would soon lead to not believing in absolute, objective truth.

So the interviewer steered the conversation away from my book and toward my own orthodoxy, which he was unsure about. His questions focused on my personal beliefs—test questions, you'd call them. Test after test followed, and although I apparently didn't flunk, he never felt comfortable enough about me to shift back to talking about the book. I wondered if he was trying to protect his listeners from me and would rather expose me than let my ideas be given a hearing on his show.

Soon I found myself feeling physically shaky, and my voice even got a little trembly. During a commercial break (for premium replacement windows at rock-bottom prices, as I recall), I wondered if interviewees were allowed to get off a live radio show early.

After the break, the radio-show host asked, "Tell me this. If you're talking to someone who doesn't believe in Jesus, will you or will you not tell him he's going to hell?"

I answered his question with a question: "Why would you want me to say that? In my experience, if you begin by condemning people, it doesn't normally make them want to believe what you believe. It makes them feel intimidated, rejected, insulted, and dehumanized." (What I didn't add was, "It makes them feel the way I feel as your guest on this show.") The experience reminded me once again how it must feel for non-Christian persons to have an overconfident, argumentative, pushy, insensitive, and domineering Christian try to "witness" to them.

As serious as the problem of overpushy witnesses may be, a related problem may be even more serious: the number of Christians who simply keep their faith to themselves and never share it with anyone. Often, these people are deeply afraid of being perceived like the radio talk-show host I met today. They don't want to be overly dogmatic. They don't want friends to run the other way when they walk into a room. They don't want to become judgmental or arrogant. They don't want to hurt anybody.

Maybe they've tried "doing evangelism" before by memorizing spiritual sales pitches, handing out leaflets, taking fake surveys, trying to "close the deal" with a prayer. And maybe they felt horrible doing so and vowed never to get close to evangelism again. They love God. They love other people. They want to help people. But they don't want to be a religious jerk, a church fanatic, or a spiritual pest—the ecclesiastic counterpart of a mealtime telemarketer or e-mail spammer barraging people with unwanted messages.

Meanwhile, there are thousands of people—no, millions—who wish they had a friend they could talk to about their questions, their doubts, their spiritual experiences, their hopes, and their prayers, answered and unanswered. But they can't risk sharing with anyone who will try to fix them, judge them, insult them, manipulate them, or otherwise treat them with something less than gentleness and respect.

So on the one side, we have people of faith, some of whom are overconfident and unwilling to listen and others who lack confidence and are unable to speak. And on the other side, we have people seeking faith who wish there were people of faith to serve as their respectful conversation partners, their gentle guides, their spiritual consultants and confidants.

Jim Henderson's book is just what all these people need. If the overconfident read it, they just might learn some sensitivity. If the underconfident read it, they may discover that life sharing—which includes faith sharing—is doable after all, that it can be a gloriously normal part of ordinary life.

And if that happens, people seeking faith will have more friends around who can help them discover what they're seeking.

I've known Jim for several years. I've been part of several of his Off The Map events and am impressed with his leadership, instincts, energy, and good humor. I've met a lot of people whose lives have been enriched and changed through Jim's influence and through the influence of those he has influenced. I know this book isn't just theory for Jim. It's the way he lives. He is exactly the kind of person spiritual seekers need to meet, but there's only one of him, and we need tens of thousands. So by reading *a.k.a. "Lost,"* perhaps you'll become the answer to somebody's first fledgling prayers: "God, please help me find someone to talk to about my questions and doubts and…"

I wasn't very successful in my radio interview today. I suppose it ended well enough; after the commercial break, the host's tone softened a bit.

"That's all the time we have. Thank you, Brian, for being with us."

"It's been a pleasure," I said, which, thinking back on it, wasn't quite honest. I stayed on the phone long enough to hear the host say,

"Now for someone I know you'll agree with…John Slate of John Slate Ford. He can meet all your new-car and used-car needs."

I'm not going to say anything snide about used-car salespeople, especially after being compared unfavorably to one. But I think we all wish that people who are sent into the world to represent Jesus Christ would be able to do so at least a little more faithfully and humanely— less like salespeople and more like the original bearer of good news. That's my prayer, and that's Jim's goal in the book you're now holding. I hope you'll read it and share it with some Christian friends. Discuss it together and try the activities and exercises Jim offers. Your life will be richer, and you'll be a blessing to the people formerly known as "lost."

—Brian McLaren, pastor (crcc.org),
author (anewkindofchristian.com),
leader in emergent (emergentvillage.com)

ACKNOWLEDGMENTS

Michelangelo didn't paint the Sistine Chapel by himself. He had lots of help. Thirteen highly qualified artists worked with him to get the job done. The truth is, no one accomplishes anything significant alone. Hillary Clinton was right—it *does* take a village. It certainly has in my case.

This book is the result of almost ten years of research by a cohort of people who passionately love Jesus and want to contribute something toward seeing his kingdom come on earth. I am one of the wealthiest people I know. I have too many good friends. Many of them helped craft this thing we've come to know as Ordinary Attempts.

People like Ken and Cherese Sutton, Rich and Rose Swetman, and Mike and Val O'Neil traipsed all over the country with me, meeting leaders and visiting churches we thought we could glean from. Others like Leigh Buchan, her daughter Ingrid, and Suzanne Timmerman contributed great stories and new ways of thinking to our little research group.

About six years ago Dave and Sharon Richards joined us. Dave and I went on to become cofounders of Off The Map, our vehicle for taking the story of Ordinary Attempts public. Sharon loves to connect with the people Jesus misses most and is one of the very best at being unusually interested in others. Frankly, without Dave's friendship, counsel, wisdom, and strategic insight, this book and the ideas found in it would not have become a reality. He has been a true partner and generous to a fault.

The Off The Map production team—Chris Marshall, Bob

Bowen, Craig Spinks, John Barce, Brent Shock and Gabe Drake, Elaine Hansen, Joe Myers, and Elizabeth DiCandilo—have helped create live events that are more like a concert than a conference and leave people feeling and thinking differently about the people formerly known as lost.

Doug Murren, Steve Sjogren, Tri Robinson, Bill Clark, and Bob McGee have greatly influenced my thinking and invested significant time in my life—for which I'm grateful. Young leaders like Ryan Beattie, Rachelle Mee Chapman, Kelly Bean, Jason Clark, Kevin Rains, and Posido, Nuc, and April Vega have graciously allowed me into their lives as a friend and have enriched me.

Todd Hunter and Brian McLaren have generously given me more time, brain power, and interest than they should have. They are two of the most respected Christian leaders on the national scene today, and I'm honored to be able to call them friends. Many of the things I've written I basically stole from one or both of them.

Sometimes good things happen to bad people. How else can I explain how this book came into being? A couple of years ago, I had the good fortune of having coffee with Kevin Miller. This was the first time we had met, and he was kindly listening to me go on and on about my ideas when suddenly a gentleman named Ron Lee walked by.

Ron was a complete stranger to me, but not to Kevin, and Kevin said, "Hey, Ron, would you be interested in a book on evangelism?"

Ron said, "Maybe, if we didn't have to use that word," at which point I spouted off, "I think I can help you with that."

Ron is a senior editor for WaterBrook Press, the publisher of this book, and has been a very helpful, creative, and encouraging guide through this project called *a.k.a. "Lost."*

Finally, I want to thank two women who have influenced me

more than anyone else in life: my mom, Jacqueline Lee Wallace, the bravest, smartest, and most articulate woman I know, and my wife, Barbara, the wisest and most authentically spiritual person I have ever known. She remains tenaciously committed to me and our accomplished children, Joshua, Sarah, and Judah.

Jesus changed my life by giving me a completely new point of view. I am proud to follow Jesus—the very best leader ever. Without him I would simply have no incentive to live.

May God use this book to inspire many redefinitions of evangelism so that ordinary Christians will regain—or perhaps experience for the first time—the fun, the passion, and the creativity that are uniquely experienced whenever we connect with the people Jesus misses most.

EVANGELISM ISN'T NORMAL

I'm convinced that I would've become a Christian at age twelve if someone had just asked me. As it turned out, another nine years passed before I heard about Jesus. A lot of bad stuff can happen to a person between the ages of twelve and twenty-one.

It wasn't that I was actively looking for God. My family was too busy surviving the daily realities of life to consider a side issue like religion. My parents survived World War II, but they couldn't survive each other. At the age of ten, I was told they would be getting a divorce. My dad never showed up to explain why our happy home was coming apart.

Mom, my three sisters, and I headed off to another type of freedom. We were now free to wonder where our next meal would come from, free to worry about paying the light bill, and free from being a typical two-parent family. And my mom was "free" to work for slave wages at a factory. It was ugly.

At age twelve I moved with my family to Portland, Oregon, where we had relatives. We rented a house there in a working-class neighborhood. Unbeknownst to me, our house was situated within walking distance of three of Portland's largest Christian organizations, one of which was Multnomah School of the Bible, filled with what must have been hundreds of "on-fire" believers just itching to tell someone about Jesus.

But I never answered a knock at the door to meet one of them. I never heard the gospel presented in our neighborhood. I didn't even know that large Christian organizations were operating in my part of town. How could my broken family have lived at the epicenter of Portland's leading Christian institutions and not have had an opportunity to hear about Jesus?

Here's how: Evangelism isn't normal. It's a program, a presentation, a memorized script. It's formalized and structured, and as a result, Christians have to work up a lot of nerve just to do it. That helps explain why most Christians only do evangelism about once a year. Then they do nothing until their church holds its next evangelism workshop.

Let's face it, traditional evangelism is simply too hard for normal Christians. It's really designed for extroverts, those with the gift of evangelism, and the few who were created to be salespeople. That leaves us ordinary types out of the game.

John Fremont was an explorer who showed people how to get to California. Everybody already knew California was there; it's just that no one knew how to get there safely.

The Pathfinder, as Fremont was called, made maps. His maps of the already known but unexplored West helped open the door for one of the greatest migrations in American history.

This book is a map of sorts. You already know about evangelism, but if you're like most people, it remains largely unexplored territory. Getting there from where you are is just too daunting, and way too strange. You need a map that shows you how to move your passion for sharing good news to a place where doing that is as normal as breathing.

Connecting with the people Jesus misses most—those formerly known as "lost"—is really not complicated. It's not even threatening. You can do it without having to memorize anything, without following a script, and without writing down a carefully prepared speech. In this book we're not going to talk about programmatic evangelism. Instead, we'll explore something that has been there all along, but that too few Christians have ventured into.

Ordinary Christians who want to connect with the people Jesus misses most need a map. We can see the destination; we just don't know how to get there. You'll be glad to know that getting there is simply a matter of living a little more intentionally. It involves being yourself and focusing on others. It's based on everyday things, such as asking questions, listening, giving away your attention, and praying behind people's backs. Each of these perfectly sane activities helps communicate the gospel. And they are things anyone can do. In fact, you're already doing them. You just didn't know it counted!

As you read this book, you'll find yourself moving a step closer to the people Jesus misses most—those who are distant from him but are more open than you think to being shown the way back to God.

CHAPTER 1

BOLDNESS IS OVERRATED

Try Free Attention Giveaways

W*itnessing.* Few words strike more fear into the heart of the average Christian.

What is witnessing, exactly, and how do you do it? What happens if you forget what to say or get tongue-tied or don't know the answer if the person asks you a question?

I know the feeling. I became a Christian at age twenty-one during the Jesus movement. Witnessing? Wasn't that something you did in court?

"Don't worry," my long-haired Jesus-people mentors told me. "We'll show you what it's all about."

They showed me the ropes of evangelizing as we witnessed our way through clouds of cannabis smoke at an outdoor rock concert.

Just a few weeks earlier, I'd been part of the "target audience." Now I was the targeter. I was told that this is what it meant to *be a Christian.* If you weren't finagling a way to steer the conversation toward Jesus, you were "selling out." If you weren't feeling uncomfortable at least once a day due to your boldness for the cause of Christ, it was doubtful that you were really saved.

When I was a new Christian protected by my closed hippie-Christian culture, it all seemed so simple. Go out, witness to as many people as you can, come back to the bible study, and tell everyone about your exploits. When you do this, you're rewarded with kudos and assurances that anyone who rejected you rejected God. You can shake that experience off like so much dirt on your shoes. Their blood is no longer on your hands. On to the next target!

In time I became a professional Christian and started acting like one. Pastors learn not to do radical things, such as walk up to people on the street and ask them for a few minutes to explain Jesus, God, sin, and hell. Instead, we find culturally appropriate ways to "present" the gospel. We do it at special church programs, or we sneak it into the talks we give at weddings and funerals. We don't want to come off like the door-to-door guys. We become more sophisticated in the way we go about sharing our faith. And sadly, many of us stop altogether.

Sure, in public we keep it up. We still remind the "troops" to go out and share the gospel with their neighbors. We read the latest demographics so that we know where our target markets are located. We even hold seminars and commit a few weeks every year to teach on evangelism. But we pretty much know that nothing is going to come of it.

I speak not as an outsider but as one who has been there and done that. I was a busy pastor, preaching, leading meetings, and coming up with mission statements. Yet I couldn't make myself stop thinking about evangelism. I couldn't live with it and I couldn't live without it. So I buried that voice.

But still I could hear it call to me. I've been intrigued, frustrated, and energized by the issue of evangelism all of my Christian life. I'm not an evangelist. I am more a student of the game we call evangelism. It may be because it's one topic that's guaranteed to irritate both Christians and non-Christians. I have been told that one of my spiritual gifts is *provocateur,* which may help explain the connection.

I'm a late bloomer. I didn't succeed in my thirties or forties. As I turned fifty I had a slight inkling as to what I wanted to do when I grew up. I took heart in studying the lives of leaders like Mahatma Gandhi, Harry Truman, and Mother Teresa, all of whom really got started around age fifty. The sense of mortality has a huge upside: It helps you stop worrying about trying to become something you aren't and get on with being who you really are—warts and all—because this is as good as it's going to get.

Someone has said, "We change when the pain of changing is less than the pain of staying the same." I finally realized that my evangelism fixation wasn't going to go away. I had buried the memory of it, but it was buried alive, and it was rising from the dead to haunt me.

You're Not Brave? Great!

Some of us are born salesmen. Most of us aren't. Some of us are born leaders, taking our place at the front of the charge and ready to accept the casualties. But again, most of us aren't. So it's a good thing that connecting with the people Jesus misses most doesn't require a Type A personality.

In his counterintuitive book *Leading Quietly,* Harvard professor Joseph Badaracco steers us away from the well-worn leaders-as-heroes path and onto the road less traveled, where ordinary people get things done. Delving into the decision-making experiences of several quiet leaders, Badaracco takes a closer look at their thinking. "The most effective leaders are rarely public heroes," he writes. "These men and women aren't high profile champions of causes and *don't want to be.*"[1]

The book of Joshua opens with these startling words: "Moses my servant is dead. Now then, you…" (1:2). Just as Joshua had to learn to lead in ways that differed significantly from Moses's approach, we have to learn to connect with the people Jesus misses most in our own way. I'm sure Joshua wanted Moses to stick around just as we want those who are more gifted than we are to go ahead and do the work of evangelizing others. But eventually it falls to us to get it done, in our own way.

Even though Moses got all the press, Joshua may have been a better leader. Moses did stuff for others; Joshua did his work through others. Moses led the Israelites across the Red Sea; Joshua followed them across the Jordan River. Moses saw the Promised Land; Joshua lived in it.

PEOPLE PREFER PRAYER

Fortunately for those of us who lack boldness, it's not all that hard to connect with the people Jesus misses most. If you can pray, you can preach. John from Mount Vernon, Washington, tells about a time he and his wife resorted to prayer:

Thirteen years ago my wife and I moved to Portland for a job. We didn't have a place to move to, so my brother offered to put us up while we looked for a house.

My brother didn't sound too hopeful [about us finding a place], especially since my job didn't start for a couple of weeks. We went out anyway and fell in love with the first place we visited. The landlord was inside painting. He asked me about the job and also asked if I had ever done that type of work before (I hadn't). He was very skeptical but accepted an application anyway, telling us he had several other applicants, all of whom he said were better prospects as tenants.... Taking applications for rentals wasn't a common practice where I came from, and I was quite intimidated by the whole process.

Anyway, we had a feeling about this, so Jeanette and I prayed that God would bring us to this man's mind every time he looked at the applications. The next morning we received a call; it was the landlord telling us he had decided to rent to us. He set up a meeting for later that morning. When we arrived, he said we would have to make arrangements for the first month's rent and deposit. We had the money to meet those requirements! Then he told us that each time he looked at the pile of rental applications, he was drawn toward ours, even though he was inclined against it from a logical point of view.

I told him we had prayed that very thing would happen. My landlord, it turned out, was something of an agnostic, but he laughed and told us that took the responsibility off him, he supposed.

Anyway, we visited our landlord and his wife when we

were down in Portland last summer. They invited us for a meal, and they prayed beforehand. It seems they had left some of their agnosticism behind.

Here's one thing John's story tell us: The people formerly known as "lost" prefer prayer to preaching. John and Jeanette weren't preachers, but they did know how to pray.

If you're not a bold evangelist, you're in the majority. In fact, you're in great company—including Saint Peter, the ultimate Green Beret who became the world's biggest Christian chicken. Under pressure he uttered curses and denied that he even knew who Jesus was (see Mark 14:66-71). At that point he had hit bottom (see Mark 14:72; Luke 22:62).

Peter was the man who boldly declared his willingness to die for Jesus (see Luke 22:33). But after the Crucifixion, he began using his leadership skills to lead the other disciples back into the fishing business. Jesus was dead, and Peter didn't know what else to do. At least fishing was something he understood.

Peter was out on the lake in a boat when he heard that familiar voice: "Come and have breakfast" (John 21:12). Immediately he knew it was Jesus. Once onshore, Peter steeled himself for Jesus's seminar on the eternal fate of compromisers and backsliders. *But it never came.*

Instead, Peter walked in on a three-part series titled "Do you love me?" Like the brilliant preacher he was, Jesus repeated himself over and over again. Some read a rebuke in these words, I assume because of the repetitive use of the phrase "Do you love me?" But if you hadn't been taught that interpretation by someone who knew ancient Greek, I would suggest that you might not have come to that conclusion. Perhaps my point of view is too hopeful, but I see it this way:

When Jesus found Peter, he didn't rebuke him; he *reminded* Peter that they loved each other and that Peter's life had purpose and meaning in serving others. Peter already knew what he should be doing. Jesus gave him the hope and motivation to do it by giving him what he needed rather than what he deserved. Cowards make great leaders when they're loved. Finding the people Jesus misses most isn't about boldness; it's about love.

ORDINARY ATTEMPTS

I resigned from witnessing in 1996. I knew I could never go back to the same old programs, the contrived joviality, or the fake evangelistic caring. But what would I replace them with?

In the church I was leading at the time, many of us decided to do what was doable and to count what really counts. We decided to count all the small attempts we made to connect with the people Jesus misses most and to do it in ways that were natural and had context in our ordinary, everyday lives. We decided to call these practices Ordinary Attempts.

An Ordinary Attempt is just what the name implies. It's something that anyone can do. You don't need special skills or experience; you just have to be aware and available. It's an *attempt*, not an accomplishment, so no extra credit is awarded for succeeding and no demerits are given for failing. Ordinary Attempts are this easy: They are nothing more than *free attention giveaways*.

People crave attention. In our cultural setting it's like the cup of cold water Jesus referred to in Matthew 10:42, where he said, "If anyone gives even a cup of cold water to one of these little ones because he is my disciple...he will certainly not lose his reward." When we *pay attention* to people because we want to nudge them toward Jesus, it refreshes them. It becomes the connecting bridge between them and God. Best of all, instead of *asking* them for something—their time, attention, and interest—we *give* them something—our time, attention, and interest. We serve them a small taste of Jesus's desire to attend to them.

This attempt to connect with the people Jesus misses most *is* evangelism. Here is my paraphrase of Matthew 10:42:

> If anyone…even cowards for Jesus
> Gives even…small things *are* the big things
> A cup of cold water…ordinary things are the *real* things
> Because he is my disciple…good intentions count too
> He will not lose his reward…it counts, and God will multiply
> its effectiveness.

Jesus made it clear that when people see him, they've seen the Father. This is what I see when I look at Jesus and, through him, his Father:

- He asked great questions.
- He wasn't frenzied when it came to moving people closer to the kingdom.
- He operated in a relatively small geographical and cultural space.
- "Sinners" found him approachable. They liked him.

I want to be like Jesus. I want to be friends with the people Jesus misses most, the people formerly known as "lost." I want missing people to like me, to want to hang out with me. I want to partner with Jesus in seeing them cross the starting line into the kingdom of God.

Christians are the freest people on earth. Our past, present, and future are completely secure through the love of Jesus. Not only do we have eternal security; we have *internal security*. In a word, we have nothing to lose. We can risk, attempt, and fail, and we'll still go to heaven.

When it comes to evangelism, we can be our ordinary selves, and it turns out to be good enough. It turns out that all Jesus needs are the five loaves and two fish of our lives—something we *already* have. Rather than trying to escape the ordinary, we should exploit it and attempt something small for God, something ordinary.

Here's an Ordinary Attempt my wife and I got involved in while in a grocery store. See if you think it counts as evangelism.

A woman ran up to the checker just as our items were moving down the conveyor belt.

"Can I get a calling card?" she asked, clearly frazzled. "My son is stuck in Italy, and his phone card won't work, so he can't call his credit-card company to get his debit card to work."

"Man, been there, done that," we said. My wife and I let the woman cut in front of us. *Should I offer to pray for her? No, that would be too weird,* I thought. She got a calling card and headed off, and we continued getting our purchases scanned.

But I did pray for her, secretly. I hoped she would come back just one more time. Surprisingly, she returned to ask the clerk for a little more help.

"What's your son's name?" I inquired.

"Colin. He's in Italy and…" She had that scared-parent look.

"Listen, I'll pray for him."

"You'll what?"

"I'll pray for Colin that he gets out of Italy."

A warm smile spread across the woman's face. "Thank you!" she said and left the store. That took all of ninety seconds.

You might be wondering: *Just how does that count as evangelism?* I would have wondered the same thing several years ago, and I still find myself wondering even now. But…what are the odds that the worried mother has *ever once* had someone stop her in a grocery store and spontaneously offer to pray for her? For that matter, when was the last time it happened to you? Since Jesus and I are partnering and he had already been working in the woman's life, I simply offered a "cup of cold water" to her and then left it up to Jesus to do the hard part of bringing her closer to his kingdom. And I really believe he will.

ATTEMPTING THE ORDINARY

Throughout this book we'll tell the stories of people who are practicing Ordinary Attempts. And at the end of each chapter, you will find suggestions for ways you can begin to connect with others in perfectly ordinary ways. These ideas can also be used with a partner, in a small group, or with your prayer group.

To begin, here are two ideas that will make your evangelistic life easier, especially if you're not the bold type.

- This week, ask someone this question: "How are you?" Now here's the tricky part. When the person begins to answer, actually listen. Don't interrupt with your own story. Spend a few minutes being unusually interested in the person, and leave it at that. Don't witness, preach, or say anything religious.

- For those who find that idea too risky, try this: Practice noticing the people God has put around you. Here's how: Take a small notebook or tape recorder with you this week and begin to write down observations (or record oral notes) about the people you notice whom you've never "seen" before—kind of like relational peripheral vision. Ask God to give you new ideas about how you could serve these people. Doing this will give you time to warm up to the "How are you?" question above.

CHAPTER 2

THE PEOPLE FORMERLY KNOWN AS "LOST"

What's in a Name

The Titans, Huskies, Giants, Razorbacks. Teams take on names they hope will create a larger-than-life image in the minds of their opponents, thus giving them a psychological edge. Labels and names and categories aren't just convenient systems for organizing life and helping to order the world around us. They are systems of ranking that convey power and powerlessness, blessing and judgment, superiority and inferiority. If you played football, you'd much prefer to make the roster for the Lions than the Kittens.

If you're old enough to remember the fall of the Berlin Wall, you might also remember the annual May Day parades in Moscow, which the USSR used as an opportunity to showcase its military might. The parade marshals were overweight Russians wearing big coats and funny hats, watching huge masses of men—known as the Red Army—

march past. The men marching in formation looked big and powerful, and their name sounded tough: the Red Army. Most of us wouldn't
want to take the field against the Red Army.

Now picture the same May Day parade with the Soviet Union
rolling its biggest missiles past Red Square to impress the rest of the
world. And here come the soldiers marching in tight formation. But
this time it's not the Red Army; it's the Pink Guys. Doesn't have quite
the same effect, does it? Just doesn't sound tough.

What nation worth its salt would allow itself to be pushed around
by the Pink Guys?

A Question of Perception

When the congregation I was leading resigned from force-feed evangelism a few years back, we also decided to rename the people we
wanted to connect with. We realized that calling people who are outside the faith "the lost" sets up an us/them dichotomy, artificially sep-
arating "the found" from those who are hopeless in their "lostness." It
also conveys a class system, setting up the assumed superiority of "the
found" in contrast to the sad plight of "the lost." Rather than one beggar telling another beggar where to find bread, the idea of "reaching
the lost" sets up an unnecessary and unhelpful obstacle.

I wanted the people in my church to *want* to be with "lost"
people, not out of a sense of duty, but of adventure and partnership
with God. I wanted them to *love* people who didn't know Jesus, not
to be mad at them for not wanting to come to church. I wanted to
change our perception of those we typically treat as outsiders in the
hope that people in the congregation would experiment with finding
new ways of connecting with them. I wanted Christians to blur the

lines between "us" and "them" the same way Jesus did. My first customers were "the found." If I couldn't reach them, I wouldn't be able to reach through them to *the people Jesus misses most.*

I realized I had more a problem of perception than of motivation. Rather than giving another speech about *why* we needed to connect with those formerly known as "lost," I needed to help Christians re-imagine *who* they were trying to connect with. We needed to overhaul how Christians perceive non-Christians.

You might be wondering, *If those who don't know Jesus aren't "the lost," then who are they?* My congregation and I tried out all sorts of new terms, and the one that proved to be the "stickiest" was *missing persons.* Author and pastor Brian McLaren likes to say, "Missing people aren't bad; they're just not where they're supposed to be." When you change their name, you change how you *feel* about them. Since in reality we do what we feel, not what we think, this small change proves to be very helpful in getting all of us back into the game of nudging people across the starting line toward Jesus.

CONTROLLING METAPHORS

A number of years ago, my wife and I were part of a counseling training program. The man who led the class was a really wise person who said stuff you pretended to understand and then later asked your wife, "What in the world did he mean by that?"

The one idea from that instructor that I never forgot was this: Change a person's metaphor, and you can change that person's life. Every one of us lives according to controlling metaphors that determine our thinking about ourselves, others, and life in general. A basic metaphor is seeing life as a glass that's half-full or half-empty.

Controlling metaphors color our thinking, and this is especially true for those of us whose Christian formation included repetitive references to "the lost." For her book *Terror in the Name of God,* Harvard professor Jessica Stern researched the primary causal factors that enable fundamentalists of every religious stripe to kill others in the name of God. One of the key factors is their ability to "dehumanize their adversaries."[1] Militant Palestinians justify killing Israeli children because in Israel everyone has to serve in the army. Consequently, when an Israeli child is killed, there is one less future soldier living in Israel.

Christians also are known to buy into this dehumanizing practice. Remember when a self-described born-again Christian shot and killed a physician who was performing abortions? The killer rationalized his homicidal action by saying he was protecting the unborn children that the doctor would have aborted in the future. How is that significantly different from the militant Palestinian viewpoint?

Christians also do violence to others in their minds when they refer to the people Jesus misses most as "the lost." They're not Jeff and Susan and Bill and Maria. They're not fellow humans; they're something else—"the lost." It's almost as if they're from another planet. We say we love them, but we act like they disgust us.

Marketers are familiar with the challenge of seeking creative ways to change how the customer "sees" a product. Perception is reality, even when the accepted perception is erroneous. Is Coca-Cola really "the real thing"?

Our perceptions determine our attitudes and actions. As I said earlier, I want Christians to *want* to be with the people Jesus misses most, not out of a sense of duty, but of adventure and partnership with God. I want Christians to *love* people who don't know Jesus, not be mad at them for not believing the right things.

BACK TO THE BIBLE

You might be booting up your computer right now so you can send me an e-mail reminding me of Jesus's parables regarding the lost coin, the lost sheep, and the lost son. In those parables, a seeking woman, a tender shepherd, and a loving father go to great pains to seek out an object, animal, or person who is lost. "If Jesus didn't see anything wrong with referring to those who are separated from him as being 'lost,' why is it wrong for Christians to think that way?" might be the tenor of your question.

Here's how I see it. In Luke 15, Jesus gave three illustrations in which a coin, a sheep, and a person go missing. They are "lost," but they also are missing. It all depends on your point of view. In the opening illustration we find a shepherd who has lost one of his sheep. The interesting thing to notice is that the shepherd feels responsible for having lost the sheep. "Suppose one of you has a hundred sheep *and loses one of them*," (verse 4). Jesus implied that the welfare of the sheep is the responsibility of the shepherd.

But what if Jesus had been looking at this situation through the eyes of a twenty-first-century evangelical Christian? In that case, he might have said: "Suppose one of the sheep wandered off and *got lost?*" Even though we assume (correctly, I believe) that the sheep in this story did, in fact, wander off because of its own stupidity, Jesus placed the responsibility on the shepherd. In doing so he gives us a glimpse into the heart of God. He suggests that God personally loves and misses every one of us, even though we've gotten ourselves in hot water. When a sheep wanders off, God feels that *he* has lost the sheep.

As a father I can easily identify with this image. If one of my kids were to get lost, my overwhelming emotion would be not annoyance but the fear that I might not be able to find my son or daughter. That puts the idea of being lost, or of finding those who have been lost, in a completely different light. With a new controlling metaphor, using Jesus's parables as a guide, we begin to look very differently at the people who are missing—those formerly known as "lost."

How about the lost coin? We read: "Suppose a woman has ten silver coins and loses one" (Luke 15:8). The missing coin is incapable of "getting lost"; it has no self-awareness or volition. Its lostness is simply another way of stating that it has gone missing. Again, the point of the story is to highlight the motivation of the one who is seeking the lost object, not to objectify the thing that is lost—which is what we have done with our term *the lost.* The woman missed the lost coin. The coin, like many "lost" people I have interviewed, had no sense of being lost. Likewise, asking people to "feel" lost is useless. It is only as they return to the loving grip of Jesus that their "feelings" of lostness return. It is our job to get them close enough to Jesus so they can regain their sense of spiritual feeling. I never felt lost until I felt Jesus missing me. When that moment came, I recognized my lostness, and I accepted his invitation to enter into his heart and life.

So far Jesus used an animal and an inanimate object to illustrate how far he is willing to go to retrieve us. He culminated his trilogy of the missing with the well-known story of a human being who loses his way. This time, unlike the first two examples, the son willfully chooses to get lost. If there is anyone deserving of being called a name, it's the prodigal: "The younger son got together all he had, set off for a distant country and there squandered his wealth in wild living" (Luke 15:13).

Here is the poster child of lostness, a willful human being running from God. The prodigal finally runs out of food and heads home.

Now the stage is set for his father to tell him why he is such a loser. You know, something *we* would want to say, like, "You idiot!" But we read that the father, rather than mentioning anything about his son's lostness, instead chooses to celebrate his son's "foundness."

Sometimes I feel that Christians are angry with lost people. We secretly want to call them names. And in many of our private conversations, we do just that. Jesus never once did that.

It is true that the prodigal was technically lost, but from the father's point of view, he was *missed.* The father's response demonstrates the heart God has toward those who snub him or, like Saint Peter, openly reject him. While we may find this kind of love irrational, it comes in handy when *we* are the ones returning home. I'm glad that the Father of Jesus saw me not as a loser (even in my lostness) but as someone he missed. I felt that loving embrace, and I came home.

Lost or Missing?

You remember the scenes from September 11, 2001. Within a few brief hours (it seemed like minutes) of the Twin Towers crumbling before our eyes, relatives, friends, and co-workers were displaying photographs of their loved ones.

The towers were obliterated, but not the memories of those who were now missing. Friends and family members, who were waiting for word of their loved ones, held up the images wherever they could find a news camera.

Missing...John.

Missing...Sarah, Frank, and Chris.

Missing...my dad.

As I watched in stunned admiration of their tenacity and love, I thought, *Those people aren't missing; they're dead. They're lost!* But then I realized that their loved ones couldn't bring themselves to call missing friends and family "lost."

Lost is final. *Lost* means defeat. *Lost* means all hope is gone. As I watched the television news, I could call these people lost because I didn't know any of them. I could call them lost because they weren't real people to me; they were victims of a terrible tragedy. I could call them lost because it was easier for me emotionally.

But those who loved the people working at the World Trade Center called them "missing" for only one reason: They *loved* them.

ATTEMPTING THE ORDINARY

Jesus asked great questions. We often assume it was to make a point or maybe even to put the other person on the spot. But I wonder if Jesus didn't ask some of his questions because he was genuinely interested in how the person would answer. Remember, Jesus misses those who are far from him. You'd never guess what you can learn from the people formerly known as "lost" until you ask a few questions.

Getting Started

Jesus set up most of his interactions with questions. He engaged the Samaritan woman in a dialogue, and when she attempted to turn it into a debate, he resisted. Finally, when the time was right, he made his point by asking a question: Why don't you go get your husband? At that, the woman began to open up even more. Jesus was preaching, but he was using questions to do the heavy lifting.

To help you come up with great questions, in the tradition of Jesus, I suggest you think about new types of questions. Many of us lack the skill and confidence for asking questions. Out of our desire to give people their privacy, we often say nothing. We feel that the oft-used evangelism question "If you died tonight…" is too intrusive—and negative. Ask that question nowadays, and it will probably be the last question you get to ask.

With that in mind, check out the following survey. The questions are fun and fast and are useful in making a connection with someone when you don't know how to get the conversation going. The survey takes about sixty seconds. Try it this week and see what happens. Notice what you learn from the experience as you connect with those formerly known as "lost."

The Four-Question Spirituality Survey

Ask someone if you can do a quick survey with no strings attached. If the person agrees, tell him or her that it will take about sixty seconds; then ask one or all of the following questions. But don't react to the answers.

- What is the difference between religion and spirituality?
- Who is a spiritual person you admire?
- If Christians would listen, what would you tell them?
- Has anyone ever tried to "save" you?

After the person answers these questions, say "thank you" and let him or her go without doing any preaching. Take note of the answers and pray a short prayer for the person.

CHAPTER 3

ORDINARY MAKES A COMEBACK

Maybe We Aren't the Problem

The ad for the cruise with the beautiful people, sumptuous food, and warm sunsets wraps with the words "Escape the ordinary." The siren song teases us with its familiar tune: "Ordinary people are boring. Be cool—float with us."

The church has its own ad for escaping the ordinary. On Sunday mornings, put-together people parade across platforms and stages, exhorting us to be extraordinary. To be people who accomplish unusual deeds for God.

Can you imagine a testimony service during which a mom got up and told how she listened to a neighbor across the backyard fence or about the time she was unusually kind to the grumpy elderly woman she runs into regularly at the store? This is supposed to inspire me?

You were *kind?* C'mon! Where's the sizzle, the special effects? What's church without stories of the glorious handful doing what the rest of us not only don't want to do but couldn't possibly do because our ordinary lives keep interrupting our appointment with destiny?

Extraordinariness is often held aloft as the goal of every right-thinking, right-believing Christian. But those ordinary folks who have taken a look behind the curtain can finally say it: "Extraordinariness is bankrupt." It has overpromised and underdelivered. I've been on this planet for fifty-six years and in church at least once a week since I was twenty-one, and I have yet to see the much-promised "revival" break out or maintain any lasting effect on God's people. In spite of my very best efforts at pastoral care, I have yet to ignite the fire of spiritual passion in more than a handful of people during any twelve-month period. I have aimed high, worked hard, practiced skills, studied programs, and developed strategies and still have come out of it with not a lot to show for my efforts.

Can you relate?

Not that many years ago, I slipped back into wondering if Jesus would ever think that my being my real self could ever be good enough to help move the kingdom of God forward in my little world. Will Jesus ever use me to move others closer to him, or do I simply lack the requisite charm, good looks, and smooth manner? Can an ordinary guy from Seattle really be useful in the kingdom, or am I too lacking in the basic essentials?

We don't usually say these things aloud, and we rarely find the words even to express our silent frustration to ourselves. "I'm just a regular, ordinary person who loves God and would love to do something for his kingdom. Too bad I'm not unusual, extraordinary, or even consistently courageous. If that's what it takes to get evangelism done, I'll just write a check." And that's what the majority of Jesus's followers do every Sunday. They listen to an extraordinary speaker, applaud when he or she is done, and write a check, the lowest form of commitment in any organization.

So before you skulk off into obscurity, let me raise your spirits with some good news: The people of Jesus are regular, ordinary people. They are normal folks, living truly *unremarkable* lives. But these are also the selfsame people who get things done!

KEEP IT SIMPLE

The U.S. Army general with the most real-life battlefield experience in World War II was "Vinegar" Joe Stillwell. He should have been a famous general, but life didn't play out according to his strategic plan. He began his military career in China but eventually ended up in California instructing reservists who had day jobs but would soon find themselves firing real guns.

Simplicity was the key to Stillwell's success. He distilled three essentials from his training: move, shoot, and communicate.

He taught that in warfare "anything that can go wrong will go wrong." Have you ever found that to be true when you thought you had the speech together and the stage set to talk to your friend about Jesus? His car breaks down on the way to meet you, his boss asks him to work late, or he just isn't in the mood to talk about spiritual stuff.

Stillwell's advice should be heeded by those of us who want to find a way to connect with the people Jesus misses most. It won't get done using fancy tactics. If ordinary people can't do it using ordinary means, ordinarily it won't get done.

So forget the speech, the pitch, and the program. Practice being ordinary. Normal people are the ones who get the important things done.

It's Always the Infantry

Allow me one more war illustration. War exposes very quickly how people respond when things *really* don't go as planned. D day was the turning point in World War II. It was planned down to thirty-second increments. Thirteen thousand planes and the largest armada of ships ever gathered were committed to the invasion. Bombs were supposed to wipe out the enemy, opening the way for Allied ground forces to land and push back the German army.

That was the plan. But if you saw the movie *Saving Private Ryan*, you know how it actually turned out. The bombs missed the forward German troops. The Allied troops fought to reach the beach under fierce enemy fire. Those who made it to dry land were simply glad to be alive. Most of the commanding officers were killed, so it was left to an ill-prepared and underequipped infantry—the "normal" people—to take the attack to the enemy.

Cringing in fear, cold and wet, and many of them without weapons, those who survived the Normandy landing managed to find a place to find shelter from the deadly machine-gun fire. At the base of the cliffs, they waited for replacements. The problem was that waiting and hiding wasn't their assignment. Getting to the top of the cliffs and taking out the machine guns was.

No one could see a way to the top except a rabbit hunter from Montana.[1] He noticed faint trails in the grass that led to the top of the bluff. Hunting rabbits had trained him to notice seemingly insignificant details that others overlooked. He led his men up the hill, eventually taking out the deadly machine-gun nests.

Maybe We Aren't the Problem

How will we win this struggle for the hearts and lives of the people Jesus misses most if ordinary Christians don't find a way to get back into the game? Why would God make evangelism so hard? Is it really just our laziness and self-focus that keep us on the sidelines, or might it be that the methods and approaches we've been offered feel too much like a sales pitch?

The church has spent enormous amounts of time and energy planning programs for reaching the unchurched. We've redesigned church parking lots, reprinted our brochures, repainted our Sunday-school rooms, and even gotten flashy Web sites up and running, but the battle isn't happening in our buildings. It's in our backyards.

The pitch and presentation sound fine as long as we're just rehearsing them in the safety of a classroom. But get me out in the workplace or talking to my friend at Starbucks, and it falls out of my head.

Maybe *we* aren't the problem. Maybe we've simply been staring at the problem for so long that we've gotten stuck using methods and approaches that ordinary people can't use. The infantry stays on the ground. They don't buzz overhead in high-tech fighter-bombers. Maybe we don't need a new, improved version of what already hasn't worked in the past.

We need a completely new approach that ordinary Christians can easily remember—because there's nothing to memorize.

CONNECTING IS EVANGELISM

Albert Einstein said, "The formulation of a problem is often more essential than its solution." What is our problem with evangelism? What is keeping us on the sidelines? Maybe it's pressure to *close the deal* with people, and we haven't been shown the value and importance of simply *connecting* with people in a normal, ordinary way.

Major-league baseball player Darin Erstad finished with 240 hits in the 2000 season. The all-time record for hits in a single season at that time was 257, held by George Sisler. Asked if there was any point during the season when he thought he might break Sisler's record, Erstad replied, "No, because I don't ever focus on that type of stuff. I just focus on taking good swings. I don't focus on results as much as the process of getting there.... You can't will hits to come. You just put the ball in play and see what happens."[2]

Erstad's goal was to simply connect with the ball—a "good swing" as he calls it. He wasn't thinking about where the ball would end up.

Why do most people who do evangelism—not to mention the people who have evangelism done to them—hate the process? If sales-strategy evangelism, the approach designed to "close the deal," is truly the biblical default mode, why don't we have a more conclusive picture from scripture of Jesus using this approach?

Where in the Gospels do we see Jesus "ask for the order"? Where do we observe him closing the deal? Why did he walk away from so many promising evangelistic opportunities, leaving only a few vague instructions behind? And why did he answer so many questions with questions instead of laying out a clear presentation of the gospel? In the Gospels we see Jesus proclaiming the kingdom of God and, at times, inviting people to follow him.

Mission to the Missing

Matthew 9 could be subtitled "Mission to the Missing." In this chapter we find several examples of Jesus crossing cultural, economic, religious, and gender boundaries as he passionately pursued the people he missed most, the ones who had never heard that he *liked them.*

As we watch him connect with the missing, pay special attention to "what Jesus *didn't* do" (WJDD), and ask yourself this question: If Jesus had been "properly" trained in evangelism and discipleship, what *should* he have done in these situations?

In Matthew 9, we see a few men bring their friend, a paralytic, to Jesus. Luke's account of this event tells us that the men actually broke through the roof of a house to get a front-row seat for their friend.

Have you ever been part of a search-and-rescue party, taking time off work and possibly risking your life for a complete stranger? Maybe you've risked your professional reputation and gone to bat for a co-worker you think deserves a raise or a new opportunity.

What motivates someone to replace self-interest with what is best for another person? Respect? Honor? Desperation? Love? We can assume that this small group was probably experiencing a mix of these same emotions.

"When Jesus saw their faith, he said to the paralytic, '…Your sins are forgiven'" (Matthew 9:2). When you miss someone you pursue that person. In this case, the sick man's friends "presented him" to Jesus. They missed seeing him in good health. They missed seeing him have a normal life. So they pursued Jesus on his behalf.

Jesus evidently saw this man as part of a group. While this type of thinking is anathema to Western individualistic-salvationism (every man and woman for him- or herself), it was common in Jesus's culture for a group to make a decision. This might help explain Jesus's response to the friends' action. He saw that the paralyzed man had the same kind of faith his friends had. In our cultural context we might express this as "if he's good with you, he's good with me." Jesus was able to read the unspoken intentions of the sick man's friends. They *announced* their intentions through their actions. In turn, Jesus *announced* his intention: to absolve the man of his sins.

When you miss someone, you *make* things happen. Perhaps caught up in and inspired by the aggressive love of the paralyzed man's friends, Jesus took the risk of *announcing* God's free gift of love without any qualifications. He decided to *make* things happen for this man. When we love people, we take risks and do irrational things. Western evangelicalism has attempted to turn the very messy process of spiritual birth into a sanitized, tightly scripted experience. Jesus loved people and engaged in the drama and spontaneity of the process.

Jesus *didn't*. . .

- close the deal by asking the man to pray "the sinner's prayer."
- wait to be asked before he offered the man forgiveness.
- ask any qualifying questions about the man's spiritual background.
- first verify the man's intention to follow him before he healed him.
- mention anything about reading the Torah or memorizing scripture.
- identify the most spiritual person in the man's group and ask that person to do some follow-up with the new convert.

If a structured approach that centers on a spiritual sales pitch is the best strategy for evangelism, then why aren't followers of Jesus naturally wired to do it? Why would God require a particular model for ministry and then equip so few of his people to succeed in using that model?

Let's find a way to nudge others toward God by using a simple approach that requires no special skill or giftedness, no superior knowledge, and no detailed training. Let's find out how to connect with the people Jesus misses most.

ANOTHER MUNDANE MOMENT

Several years ago, when my wife and I lived in Ohio, we went shopping on a Saturday night. While Barb was trying on dresses, I struck up a conversation with the salesclerk. I noticed she was from Latin America, so I began asking questions about her home country. One question led to another, and I found out that this was a second job for her. Her real job was as a sales manager for a large hotel. It turned out that she was divorced and her son spent the weekends with his dad, so she found a second job working in a department store to keep her occupied on weekends.

The thought crossed my mind: *She's working a second job to kill her loneliness. I should invite her to church.*

What would you do at that point? Would the thought of asking a salesclerk to attend your church seem too weird? Probably. But what if you were just being yourself? You've met a woman who appears to be lonely, a person who would welcome some friendship.

I'm not suggesting being pushy and obnoxious. But what stops us from just naturally inviting people to church, or inviting them to know Jesus after we've known them for a while? What stops you from asking people if you could pray for them when they express a need, a

worry, or a concern? Why do we find it so hard to just be our authentic, spiritual selves?

I felt that this woman was lonely, so I really had no choice but to
invite her to church. When I did, I found out that several of her
friends had already invited her to our church. She said, "There's something there for me!" I gave her my business card, and later my wife
and I stopped by the store to see her again.

Connecting with this woman was as simple as asking questions,
listening to her answers, and sensing a need. Finding the people Jesus
misses most involves doing the most ordinary thing you can do: Being
yourself.

ATTEMPTING THE ORDINARY

Here's a simple way to develop *the art of noticing*. I learned this from my wife, who developed a spiritual discipline she calls Momentology. It's the practice of making a big deal out of the moments one experiences in life. I experience a "moment" whenever I get all the bills paid for the month (especially the mortgage). In Momentology, we learn not to let those moments slip past unnoticed, but rather to milk them for all they're worth.

This week, pay special attention and keep track of your moments. Call another Momentologist and share your story with him or her. As you do this, you'll be practicing the spiritual art of noticing. When you can notice God in your own life, it's easier to recognize him in someone else's. If you can make a big deal out of small stuff in your life, it will be more natural for you to do the same for others.

As you practice Momentology, you'll start noticing the stories of others—including the stories of missing people—and you'll naturally celebrate their lives. Even the ordinary stuff. This is a great way to connect with the people Jesus misses most. No special skills required.

CHAPTER 4

THE GOSPEL ACCORDING TO YOU

Practice Being Yourself

As you know, Jesus didn't have one standard approach to evangelism. Nor did he leave us an explicit set of instructions regarding this important practice. What he did leave us were stories, and in these stories we discover his recipe for evangelism. But like all recipes, there is room for personal preference and expression. (I guess that's why there are fifty ways to make a chocolate cake.)

Jesus advocated two basic evangelism practices. He said we should *speak* the gospel: "Preach the good news to all creation" (Mark 16:15). He also instructed us to *serve* the gospel: "Whatever you did for one of the least of these brothers of mine, you did for me" (Matthew 25:40). It is at the intersection of these two practices that we discover what "truly personal" evangelism looks like.

Most of us have been taught to focus on just one of these passages, but in mixing them together, we practice being ourselves and discover just how attractive that is to the people Jesus misses most. It really intrigues them.

AT THE INTERSECTION OF OPPOSITES

In the early 1700s, John Harrison invented the chronometer, an instrument that enabled ships to accurately measure longitude—something astronomers had tried to do for several hundred years using the stars. Sailors knew that if they could tell time at sea, the problem would be solved. To find your ship's longitude, you would simply compare the time on the ship against London time. The problem is that no one believed it was possible to invent a clock that could withstand the rigors of conditions at sea.

But Harrison did it by combining two kinds of metals: brass and steel. It was the combination of these two very different metals that made it possible for a clock to operate in all types of weather. When one metal contracted, the other would expand. The clock could continue to function without interruption. Ships could accurately locate their position, and the British Empire could expand to the point that the sun would never set on one of her colonies without rising on another. Brass and steel, two very different types of metal, were combined, and whole new shipping routes opened up, enabling the British Empire to spread its way of life all over the world.

Small discoveries lead to big changes. New ideas often emerge when we combine approaches that at first seem opposed to one another.[1]

Preach to Serve and Serve to Preach

I think of the opposing approaches of evangelism like this: We should preach as if we're serving and serve as if we're preaching.

We preach as if we're serving when we use words that carry people's hearts to Jesus rather than just correcting their mistaken beliefs. We preach as if we're serving when we refuse to steer the conversation in a direction that satisfies our own agenda. We preach as if we're serving when we ask more questions than we give answers. We preach as if we're serving when, after someone asks us what we're about, we talk about Jesus in a way that is real and matches their level of receptivity. We preach as if we're serving when our hearts' intention is for the other person to experience Jesus's love and reality, not just hear our beliefs.

And here's the other approach. We serve as if we're preaching when we do things for others, putting their needs ahead of our own. We serve as if we're preaching when we restrain ourselves from verbally clarifying that our *real* motive is to demonstrate God's love. We serve as if we're preaching by anticipating our missing friends' level of interest and praying behind their backs, asking Jesus to nudge them toward a heartfelt relationship with him.

If this sounds complicated, as if it's leading up to a detailed action plan or some big strategy you'll need to memorize, relax. Here's another way of saying all of this:

- Be yourself.
- Be human.
- Be normal.
- Be real.
- Be intentional.

When we combine these two approaches—serving as if we're preaching and preaching as if we're serving—we're able to expand Jesus's kingdom further into the hearts of the people Jesus misses most.

THE ART OF BEING REAL

Jesus was a walking lesson in how to connect with missing people and still keep it real. He preached to serve and served to preach. He wove these two opposites together like jazz trumpeter Miles Davis did when he intersected sterling technique with brilliantly constructed improvisation. Jesus lived intentionally but could "play" with whatever life handed him and use it to write his song of love on the hearts of the people he missed.

Mission to the Missing

One day Jesus was walking in his village and had an encounter with the local customs officer. In that encounter, Jesus elegantly navigated a series of unique cultural twists and turns, recruited a key disciple, and interacted with his "tribe" without once *forcing* an opening for a spiritual conversation. He kept things real and made a connection with the people considered by others to be hopelessly *lost*.

"While Jesus was having dinner at Matthew's house, many tax collectors and 'sinners' came and ate with him and his disciples" (Matthew 9:10). Here's the sequence we see in this story:

1. Jesus said, "Follow me" (Matthew 9:9).
2. Matthew followed Jesus.
3. Jesus followed Matthew (to his house).

You tell me: Who, exactly, is following whom? I thought Matthew was supposed to drop everything and become a spiritual hippie for

Jesus. I assumed that Jesus would lead him off to be immersed in a heavy program of discipleship. I didn't envision Jesus turning to Matthew and saying, "Hey, before we start doing important ministry stuff, let's drop by your place."

Jesus then stayed at Matthew's house just long enough to give his enemies (the religious leaders) the ammunition they needed to justify their suspicions. When you miss people, you follow them into *their* world. Jesus took the risk of being misinterpreted, misunderstood, and misquoted because he loved those who were missing.

Jesus didn't ask Matthew to take a class on "inviting and including." Instead, he immediately entered Matthew's world. Jesus had a habit of following his friends home rather than asking them to come to his place. There is also no record of Jesus giving a "spiritual speech" at Matthew's house. We've been taught that *real* evangelism means leveraging relationships so we can "get the word out." But we don't see that in Jesus's model. For Jesus, just being with the missing was a sermon.

Following Jesus on his mission to the missing means *we go to them*. We spend time with them in their cultural context, just as we ask them to spend some of their time in a new cultural context. We don't spell out every detail of the plan of salvation. Many of them are already listening closely. They are interacting with and wondering about the Living Plan of Salvation, Jesus, who expresses himself through Christians just being themselves.

Here is what Jesus *didn't* do (WJDD):

- He didn't instruct Matthew to join the Jesus commune.
- He didn't have Matthew pray the prayer "just to be sure."
- He didn't discourage Matthew from spending time with his old friends by sharing the verse about bad company corrupting good character.

- He didn't challenge Matthew to give his personal testimony at the dinner.
- He didn't even make Matthew pay back all the people he had ripped off, as Zacchaeus did in Luke 19.

Ever Heard of Lyme Disease?

Lyme disease is caused by bacteria called *Borrelia burgdorferi* (Bb). Bb is carried by the deer tick to an unsuspecting animal or person. In spite of its role as a killer, the deer tick lives a very ordinary life. Here's how the author of *Biography of a Germ* describes its daily routine:

> Finding hosts is no mean task for a creature that has no wings, cannot jump and walks like a nonagenarian. Rare is the tick that ever travels more than a yard or two from where it hatched. Its questing [the gallant term archaeologists use for "seeking hosts"] consists mostly of waiting. In exquisitely slow motion the tick trundles to where the hosts are most likely to brush against vegetation and pick up passengers, which is anywhere from several inches to several feet above the ground. Genetically programmed to move against gravity, the tick at each stage of its life trudges up stalks of grass or stems of shrubbery. Then it waits to seize a passing host with a pair of legs especially adapted for grasping.[2]

Sounds like a description of many of us, doesn't it?
- We're nonathletic.
- We're not exactly world travelers.

- We spend a lot of our time waiting.
- We often feel as though we're swimming upstream.

Nevertheless, the reason you're familiar with Lyme disease is because the lowly deer tick, in spite of its ordinariness, gets the job done. Precisely because it doesn't appear to be strong and is virtually invisible to unsuspecting targets, the deer tick has proven to be an extremely difficult enemy to contend with.

Like an ordinary deer tick that is genetically predisposed to do what it does, many of us feel genetically encoded to do *something* to nudge people toward Jesus. We keep climbing up the little blade of grass called "my life" to make ourselves available to whomever God brings by. We can't help but care about those around us. But like the deer tick, we can't fly or jump. We can't sing or dance. And most of all, we are not equipped to "preach."

Somehow we must rediscover the power and attractiveness of simply being ourselves. It turns out that just doing that is good enough to get the job done.

Practice Being Yourself

If being Christians meant we were the most *real* people on earth rather than the most religious, evangelism as a program would disappear forever. Why? Simply because the people Jesus misses most would be exposed to his message through the very natural means of friendship, kindness, concern, and listening ears. This kind of reality would surprise and mystify them instead of confusing them. Perhaps then the missing would seek *the found* to find out more about what motivates the caring nature of those who live authentic lives.

The beauty and truth of this simple, ordinary approach to connecting with others is that it doesn't get hung up on religion and rules and external trappings. There isn't a right way and a wrong way to listen intently to a friend talk about her hurts and doubts and struggles. It just takes a Christian who is willing to stop long enough to *pay attention.*

Simply put, people aren't shopping for religion; they're looking for something that's real. Jesus is at the center of reality and has commissioned us to invite others into his reality by living it and loving them. So just be yourself. That's as good as it's going to get. And when you do this simple thing, it intrigues people.

THE CIGARETTE LIGHTER ORDINARY ATTEMPT

Chris is a seminary student living in Ohio. He was working at a video-rental store when he had an opportunity to practice being himself.

> One night a man came into the store to return a video. He had long black hair and tattoos on every portion of his viewable skin, wore mostly black clothing, and reeked of cigarette smoke. While checking his movie back in, he asked me an unusual question: "What kind of Zippo do you have?" (Zippo is a popular brand of cigarette lighter that comes with different designs.) I informed him that I didn't have one but was eager to see his.
>
> His Zippo had a family of four seated around a dinner table, but they were all skeletons. He then said, "This is how I see things. We're all dead already—just waiting to die." I decided to "be myself" and see how he would react to a con-

trasting viewpoint. "That's interesting," I said, "but I'm a
Christian and think that God has more for us in this life."

I waited for him to dart for the door at the mention of
God, but just the opposite happened: He was receptive. He
said, "I just got out of prison after sixteen years for attempted
murder. 'Doing my own thing' is all I've ever known, and I let
my son do 'his own thing,' and he just dropped out of school."

I responded, "You know, I might have ended up the same
way if someone hadn't come alongside me and helped me
through some difficult times. In fact, that's one of the reasons
I'm a Christian, to help others find more in this life."

He said, "I never had that in my life. Can you help my
son? Could he come to your church sometime?" I let him
know that I would be glad to hook up with him and give him
a ride to church. Wow! A God conversation from a Zippo
question! Who would have thunk it?

MOST OF THE TIME JESUS TOOK A BOAT

Jesus is famous for walking on water, but most of the time he took a
boat. Seven hundred years before Jesus came to earth, a prophet pre-
dicted that when the Messiah appeared, no one would notice him. He
would look and act like an ordinary human much of the time. Perhaps it was his ordinariness that attracted sinners, who took to him
much more eagerly than did the religious leaders.

If you have found that programmatic evangelism isn't working for
you, give human evangelism a try. This is as simple as it gets: When
all else fails, try being yourself. Or even better, give it a try *before* all
else fails.

ATTEMPTING THE ORDINARY

At first, an outreach to naked bikers, people in drag, and costumed solstice celebrants might not seem to be an "ordinary" attempt. But after listening to Pastor Rachelle Chapman tell her story, you might change your mind:

> A mob of bikers wearing nothing but body paint are the first to come through the starting gate. Next, there's an inflatable sculpture that is having a bad hair day; men on stilts in elaborate drag, and a float full of Oompa Loompas. You'll find our religious community, ThPM, at the end of this long line of celebrants. We're pulling a forty-foot-long caterpillar. It's the Litter Bug, and we are the Trash Fairies, cleaning up the glitter and pompoms left behind by this extravaganza.
>
> This is what an Ordinary Attempt looks like when you live in the Fremont District in Seattle. The biggest deal in this part of town is the Annual Solstice Parade, which draws thirty thousand people—all there to celebrate the return of the sun. So ThPM did "church" during preparations for the parade. We brought our soup pot, broke bread, and drank wine with our neighbors. We made costumes out of recycled stuff. We asked for advice. We lent a hand.
>
> At our first build date, my husband and I had a great talk with Dulcie. She lived alone and had spent the week traveling to a really depressing town in outer Nevada, where she might have to move in order to work. We talked about the parade

and things she had built in the past. Her favorite was the time she was a dung beetle, rolling a ball of...well...you know. When we parted she said, "Thanks. I just came down because I was alone in my apartment, and I didn't want to be alone."[3]

Your city might not have a big solstice parade every year, but every city and town has some event that brings people out and gets them involved. So find a community activity you can participate in— a parade, festival, historic reenactment, town homecoming, whatever. Then be real, be yourself, and get involved by volunteering for a job no one else wants, such as picking up litter, cleaning toilets, or updating the event's Web site.

As you get involved, keep track of all the side conversations you have along the way. And as you pay attention to others, notice how even "unusual" people in your community have the usual problems.

CHAPTER 5

COUNT CONVERSATIONS, NOT CONVERSIONS

The True Size of Small Talk

Conversation is important because it's how we connect with each other. And when I mention conversation, I don't mean a lengthy, formal, practiced speech. At some point Christians got the idea that the only kind of talk that *counts* (when it comes to evangelizing) is "the speech"—you know, the contrived presentation that supposedly leads to a conversion.

Consequently, most of us rarely talk with non-Christians. Since we aren't good speechmakers, we quietly go about our business and hope no one asks us to talk about God, since we don't know enough to make "the speech." We're convinced that small talk is useless, so why bother?

THE TRUE SIZE OF SMALL TALK

People change at a certain speed, the speed of "sense making." Small talk is our delivery system for making sense of things. We chat our way to change. We "consider" whether a new idea makes sense for us. When it comes to motivating people toward deep change, *speeches* are overrated. Conversations, a.k.a. "small talk," give us the time to make sense out of our lives. In his fascinating book *The De-Voicing of Society*, John Locke discusses the important role small talk fulfills in our lives.[1] Here are some observations I gleaned from his writing:

1. *When we talk just for the heck of it, it's not just information.* We have become too utilitarian in our approach to conversation, failing to realize that the primary reward of conversation is that it builds relationships.

2. *Speaking and feeling are closely related.* When one person speaks to another, the speaker hears his or her own voice and feels more deeply the thing that is being described or explained.

3. *It's not the words...it's the heart.* The nonverbal aspects of a conversation, such as eye contact and body language, are not random, disconnected behaviors. Your heart attitude shows nonverbally even when it might not come through in your words.

4. *The impact of small talk is enormous.* "If you don't think much of small talk, try living without it for a while. One of the chief complaints of those so-called commuter marriages is the [couple's] inability to discuss the inane."[2] Like "What did you have for lunch today?" or "Who did you talk to at work today?" Relationships thrive on small talk.

CONVERSATION > COMMUNITY > CONVERSION

How do we change our minds? What is the process humans typically follow when they are moving toward significant change?

Sociologist Peter Berger has studied the connection between conversation and change on the deepest level. After analyzing Berger's findings, Asbury Seminary professor George Hunter made the following connection between conversation and spiritual conversion.

> In a pluralistic society, the possibility of *conversion,* that is, changing the way one perceives essential reality, is opened up through *conversations* with people who live with a contrasting view of reality. One adopts and internalizes the new worldview through socialization into a *community* sharing that new worldview.[3]

In other words, we change our minds about life not simply because of correct information but because we trust our conversation partners. To the degree that we are included in their community or social context and treated as insiders, we open up to their ideas.

The Gospels refer frequently to "the disciples." But have you ever tried to delineate just who exactly was included in those references? It looks as if the lines blurred fairly often when Jesus was speaking to a group of disciples. Missing people appeared frequently on the fringes, eavesdropping on many of the talks Jesus gave to his primary followers. Jesus treated those who were not yet followers as if they had every right to be there, to hear the inside story, the conversation of the inner circle. And when he spoke, he didn't bother explaining himself or asking permission of either the insiders or the outsiders.

For example, Jesus "noticed" Zacchaeus the tax collector up in a tree. Zacchaeus had been listening to Jesus from the fringes. Afterward, he took Jesus home, invited his friends over, and publicly announced that from that day forward he would follow Jesus. Cool ending, but it all started with Jesus simply "noticing" someone, acknowledging that person, and including him in his circle. Zacchaeus took it from there, responding to Jesus's free attention giveaway and giving his life to God.

THE CELTIC WAY OF EVANGELISM

In AD 432 Saint Patrick led a small band of Christians into Ireland. At that time the Emerald Isle was a land of barbarians. (Picture the army of naked guys in *Gladiator,* but hundreds of years earlier.) Patrick's team had to be creative and fast on their feet. According to professor George Hunter, the approach Patrick used was to "meet the people, engage them in conversation and ministry, and look for people who appeared receptive."[4] Hunter identifies several of the Celtic Christians' methods for connecting with their missing friends.

The Celtic Christians Treated Outsiders Like Insiders
"The number of *cultural adaptations* they managed was unprecedented," Hunter observed.[5] Celtic Christians believed that people should "belong before they believe," so Patrick and his partners included the outsiders in the life of their fellowship. Rather than plant their monastery away from the village (the traditional approach), Patrick established the community within walking distance of the village. Then Patrick and his team simply invited people in so they could see what the Christian life was all about.

The following Ordinary Attempt story, from a friend in Seattle, illustrates what this might look like today:

> One of the churches in the university district has a Thanksgiving feed every year. The organizers are friends of mine, so they have been recruiting volunteers from my real-estate office. Last year Debbie went. She indicated that the experience was pivotal in her seeing Christians in action and realizing that they weren't all weird. We now have a number of volunteers from our office working at the Thanksgiving event, and it's been a terrific time of "bonding" and fun.
>
> The volunteers get a taste of what Christians are like, and they appreciate being able to "give back." We're glad to provide the forum for them. Then we have an opportunity to talk to them on all levels. I think it's great, and it has made me rethink every time our church has a project to help the needy around us. I can ask the people I work with if they would like to join us.

The Celtic Christians Talked About Everyday Issues

Hunter points out that Christians today usually avoid talking about the very things people are most concerned about. The Celtic Christians didn't make this mistake.

> The problem is that Western Christianity usually ignores the *middle level* that drives most people's lives most of the time.... Western Christian leaders usually focus on "ultimate issues." The Celtic Christians addressed life as a whole and may have addressed the middle level more specifically, comprehensively

and powerfully than [any] other Christian movement ever has (emphasis added).[6]

It wasn't simply a matter of speaking the dialect of the local population. Patrick and his partners talked about things Celts liked to talk about, and they used Celtic icons and symbols as spiritual bridges into God-talks. The three-leaf clover is associated with Ireland because Patrick used it to talk about the Trinity.

The "middle issues" are things people talk about every day: the weather, the kids, the job, the bills. This is not programmatic evangelism, which relies on steering people into a certain conversational track. That's manipulation, not conversation. If you feel compelled to hurry a conversation along so you can get to the "ultimate issues," such as heaven and hell, you're missing the very things the other person most wants to talk about. When you take time to talk about the middle issues of life, you signal to the other person that you care about his or her life and concerns. You give the person something (your attention) rather than asking for something (a decision).

God cares about details, even small details we would often consider mere coincidence. Take Dana Colwell, from Michigan, who credits her bust-enhancing bra with more than simply an uplifting experience. Her bra, Colwell claims, saved her life.

While Colwell was cutting the grass one day, a one-and-a-half-inch nail shot out from under the lawn mower and punctured her right breast. Doctors say the injury would have been far worse had it not been for the extra padding in her "liquid-curved" Maidenform.

"If I wouldn't have put the bra on, I probably would be dead," the thirty-one-year-old said. "I love that bra! When I got up to put my clothes on, I almost didn't wear the bra. But a higher power told me to put it on."[7]

Dana Colwell's higher power was paying attention to details.

Missing people want a God who can relate to their ordinary lives. A God who will tell them what bra to put on, if need be. I'm convinced that people gravitate toward the generic "higher power" because they don't think of the Christian's God as being interested in such mundane matters. Christians, when talking about God, typically describe a God who seems much more interested in holiness than in humanity.

But the truth is that Jesus *liked* people. He zeroed in on a few things, not overwhelming his listeners with a full description of God or God's kingdom. And often, when Jesus was asked a question, he shifted attention back onto the person by asking that person a question.

Listening is a very human process. It involves learning to ask questions—to shift attention back to others, to wonder aloud about things, to not be in a hurry. *Paying attention* means we join with Jesus and feel the price he paid to restrain the urge to tell people everything he knew. Jesus was an artist when it came to conversation. There is no question that he spent much time preaching and teaching. But those were just mechanisms he employed in between conversations.

The Celtic Christians Looked for the Good

"Celtic Christianity viewed human nature not as being radically tainted by sin and evil, intrinsically corrupt and degenerate," Hunter writes, "but as imprinted with the image of God, full of potential and opportunity, longing for completion and perfection. Patrick started with the assumption that people would be receptive and he treated them that way."[8]

Patrick was very high on God's love for missing people. He assumed that God *liked* human beings, and he began conversations around *anything good* he could find in people. Their kindness, loyalty, sacrifice, earnestness, interest in others, anything! He might have approached a "Friday-night" sinner with a question as innocuous as "So, did you get a chance to see the football game or do any shopping over the weekend?" He would probably work to "catch [people] acting like Jesus," such as noticing that they gave up having one last beer so they could be the designated driver. He'd probably say, "Wow! Aren't you Irish? Now that's real friendship; what prompted that generous act?" For Patrick, the goal wasn't to wrestle people theologically to the ground. The goal was to nudge them across the starting line toward Jesus.

Conversations are fragile things because people are constantly "sniffing" to see who is safe and who isn't. Like ants sensing one another's pheromones, we use small talk to decide which relational trails we should take. Conversations are emotional on-ramps we provide one another to signal our potential interest in moving closer.

When a friend at work tells you about his weekend and mentions that he and his girlfriend spent Saturday night together getting drunk at a cabin on the lake, it could easily trigger your sin-o-meter. You might feel compelled to mention that since you're a Christian, you "aren't into that sort of thing." If you're a really on-fire Christian, you might even add that "God doesn't like drunkenness and premarital sex." While both statements are true, neither one signals to your colleague that you care about him as a friend. Instead, those statements signal "I don't want to talk to you until you change and become like me."

Jesus gave people an experience of love and reality, not a speech about it. When people experience our attention, love, and genuine interest in them, they begin to feel differently. And some will want to know what it all means. This may be what Jesus was getting at when he said that people "will know that you are my disciples, if you love one another" (John 13:35). Let the missing come among you. Include missing people in the life of your Christian community—not just at a church service but also in situations like the one described in the story earlier in this chapter. Invite missing people to serve with you, in part so they can see up close what Christians are like. Let them watch you as you live life with other Christians.

ATTEMPTING THE ORDINARY

Starting today you can begin to shift your approach from speeches to conversations, from information to relationship. But to get there takes focus and intentionality. Here are a few practical ways to get started.

1. Ask questions. Jesus got into people's heads before he got into their hearts, and he did it through questions. Conrad Gempf, author of the book *Jesus Asked,* writes, "As I re-read my gospels I noticed that they didn't portray Jesus as being incredibly smart or knowledgeable. In fact the gospels go out of their way to present a Jesus who asks lots of questions and who, in at least one notable case, doesn't know the answers of questions addressed to him."[9]

2. Make small talk. The ability to engage in small talk is huge. Don't worry that it doesn't convey important and useful information. Of course it doesn't. That's not its purpose.

Engaging in small talk is how people *smell* each other: "Does that person care enough about me to ask what I did over the weekend—and then bother to listen?" Don't be a *meaning* addict, seeking information in every verbal exchange. Be willing to be bored for Jesus. That's where the *paying* in paying attention comes in. Talk about stuff that matters to the other person—the weather, the kids, the bills, the middle stuff.

3. Practice normal talk. Too many of us have forgotten how to speak English. We talk about our "daily walk," referring to a regular devotional life and other spiritual disciplines, when most people would assume we're talking about an exercise program. If we're going to connect with the people Jesus misses most, we need to practice talking normally, which means using regular English. Here's a starter list of words and phrases that should be banned outside (and maybe even inside) your church group: quiet time; "I felt a peace about it"; hand of the Lord; put out a fleece; "I felt a real burden"; anointing; a word from the Lord; "I covet your prayers"; "I just feel so blessed"; "the Lord convicted me"; "I felt led to…"; "the Lord spoke to me"; "I sought the Lord's face." And here's my all-time favorite: "If he opens the door…"

To reveal additional instances of in-group jargon, play the Church Chat Game. See how many times group members catch one another using banned words, and then practice talking normally with one another. See which substitute words and phrases you come up with that are understandable to those you meet outside the church.

4. Say "wow." When a friend tells you something, like the story about the guy and his girlfriend, and you don't know what to say, try "Wow!" It works every time and gives you a chance to regroup. We all love hearing "wow." It's like saying, "Tell me more." Try it next time a missing person messes with your worldview.

CHAPTER 6

EVANGELIZE WITH YOUR EARS

Jesus Asked Great Questions

In a television commercial, two women are caught guy watching. They're guessing whether the guys are wearing boxers or briefs. Michael Jordan walks by, catches their collectively embarrassed eye, and says, "Hanes—let's just leave it at that."

How much did the underwear manufacturer pay Jordan to utter seven words? Lots. Why did they do it? Simple. Jordan is an attention broker. The Industrial Revolution required manpower. The Information Age required knowledge. But the current Information Overload Era requires *attention management.* Our ability to capture people's attention leads to success—or at least significant progress—in many areas of life and business. As followers of Jesus, we need to become experts in the economics of attention.

But how? In daily life we try to have an impact, but it's tough to get anyone to pay attention. Many of us pay *for* attention (some call therapists "professional friends"). Others barter for attention with a quid pro quo—"I'll listen to you for a while; then you stop talking and listen to me." This scene plays out over and over again in our daily lives. When it comes to getting attention, there are no free lunches. We pay for attention, borrow it, or loan it out with interest.

But *free* attention giveaways—who's ever heard of that?

How to Give Away Your Attention

Along with my friend and fellow idea explorer Jon Bogart, I began experimenting with new ways of approaching people. The willing participant in our experiment one day was Katy, our server at Bob Evans restaurant. We didn't have much time, so I asked Katy if she had sixty seconds to answer four questions with no strings attached. She agreed, and we began. (Warning! Don't try this unless you're ready to stop, listen, and pay attention.)

I asked Katy:

- "Can you name any of the Gospels in the New Testament?" She said she couldn't.
- "Who was the apostle Paul?" She said she didn't know.
- "What does the term *born again* mean?" She wasn't sure.
- "Has a close friend ever told you that he or she was born again?" She said that, in fact, a friend had said as much.

That was it. We thanked Katy for her answers, and she hurried off to serve other customers. Later, when she returned to refill our coffee mugs, she asked, "What are you guys into?"

"We're trying to figure out what people know about Christian stuff," Jon responded.

"Why?"

"Well, we want to help Christians learn how not to be jerks." At this Katy laughed a knowing laugh.

"Yeah," she said, "that would be helpful."

After more conversations at Bob Evans over the following weeks, Katy volunteered to appear with me at an event Jon and I were producing called Off The Map. When it was Katy's turn to speak, I asked about her experiences with Christians and church. One of her earliest church-related memories was her dad's refusal, years before, to allow her to be baptized by a certain priest, whom her dad had discovered was gay.

Think about that situation. It's representative of the kind of challenges people can run into in their search for God. Katy is not a Christian yet, but we are friends and continue to e-mail periodically. She recently told me, "You would be proud of me because I started reading the bible."

I responded, "What gave you that idea?"

She laughed. Humor goes a long way in connecting with the people Jesus misses most.

WHAT MISSING PEOPLE ARE LOOKING FOR

When Christians show genuine interest in others, people sometimes begin to believe that God might actually *like* them. The great part is that being unusually interested in people doesn't require special expertise or hours of training. In fact, it involves nothing more than living your normal life and simply beginning to practice the art of noticing those around you.

Jesus, of course, was a master at showing interest in others. As

Brian McLaren likes to say, "Jesus was long on conversations and short on sermons." Jesus's most common on-ramp to people's hearts was the practice of asking great questions.

- Who do people say I am?
- Where will we find food for these people?
- What do you want me to do for you?
- Have you had breakfast?
- Do you believe I will heal you?

In John 4, Jesus engaged the Samaritan woman in a dialogue, and when she attempted to turn it into a debate, he redirected the conversation with more questions. Finally, at the right time, he made his point with this comment: "Tell you what, go get your husband."

This left her pondering, *Who is this person? How does he know about me?* She began to open up even more, and eventually she returned to her village, saying, "Come, see a man who told me everything I ever did" (John 4:29).

We don't find any recorded evidence that Jesus went *on and on* about this woman's moral failings. Rather, he majored in great questions and minored in declarative statements. The woman's response also tells us something about Jesus's tone of voice and approach. She hurried to encourage her friends to come and meet her new friend. What person in her right mind introduces her friends to someone who's been *mean* to her?

Communication experts tell us that content comprises a mere 7 percent of our communication, while tone of voice carries 70 percent. When it comes to connecting with people like Katy or the woman at the well, using our ears is much more effective than giving a speech. Jesus teaches us that when it comes to getting through to others, listening is not only the best first step; it's the best second and third step as well.

Conrad Gempf points out that in the Gospels, Jesus "doesn't ask primarily because he wants to acquire knowledge.... He asks to help people realize where they stand; he asks questions in order to give an occasion for a reply, in order to initiate a conversation."[1]

You might be thinking Jesus had some special power as the Son of God that enabled him to get extra mileage out of his questions. But if he had that kind of power, then why would he bother to ask questions at all? He could have simply cut to the chase, told the woman at the well that she was a sinner in peril of eternal damnation, and commanded her to repent right there on the spot. But he didn't. Why?

Maybe because it's actually true that he limited himself to the kind of humanity you and I are stuck with. Maybe he wanted us to know what it would look like if we wanted to partner with God in connecting with the people he misses, in a truly human but spiritual way.

COUNT TO THREE

We can introduce people to God by using our ears. All it takes is remembering to count to three. A friend who teaches English as a Second Language (ESL) calls this three-count "wait time." Wait time is simply waiting just a pause longer than you are accustomed to when you're talking to someone.

Often after we ask someone a question, we become anxious and rush in to provide the answer. We ask the person for an answer but then fail to wait long enough for him to respond. The premise of wait time is this: People need more time to think and respond than we normally give them. According to my ESL friend, research shows that the average length of time we wait for a response is between one-half and one second. Waiting as little as another two-and-a-half seconds gives a person time to think and formulate his response. That's why we need to ask a question and then count to three.

My ESL friend tells me that the optimal length of wait time is five to ten seconds. But that's for highly motivated listeners like salespeople. (They call it "the golden silence.") Waiting five to ten seconds generates significantly higher sales, so it's worth it to salespeople to wait.

But time is not primarily money; it's attention. That's the thing everyone craves. And sadly, it's in short supply.

What this means for ordinary Christians such as you and I is that the gift of attention—asking good questions and then patiently listening—is one of the best gifts we can give. And it's amazingly simple. Ask a good question, then count to three. If you're a word person rather than a numbers person, ask a question and then silently repeat the words "Baa baa black sheep, have you any wool?" at medium tempo. Your friend will probably start to respond before you finish silently saying "wool."

If you want to influence others, you first need to earn their trust. Listening carefully to someone increases that person's trust in you. People won't allow you to influence them if they don't trust you.

If you are normally a cut-to-the-chase conversationalist, stopping long enough for the person to answer will require some practice. If salespeople and educators can learn to do this in order to influence people to buy their ideas or products, you can too. Jesus said, "The people of this world are more shrewd in dealing with their own kind than are the people of the light" (Luke 16:8). We can learn valuable skills from those shrewd folks who may not know God but who understand people.

Spiritual Formation Through Listening

If Jesus had asked a person a question only one time, that would still provide all the motivation I need to practice listening. In order for me to become more like Jesus, I must master the art of noticing, the practice of free attention giveaways, and the discipline of learning how to count to three. The best part is that while these spiritual practices might be challenging, they are decidedly *doable*. And it's not just about the impact on others. My own spiritual formation depends upon my commitment to listen to the people Jesus misses most.

For your own spiritual development, as well as to help you introduce others to God, free attention giveaways will enable you to do the following:

- Create a niche in your missing friend's life as being "someone who really cares." (Certainly an improvement over "that guy who can't shut up.")
- Grow spiritually by *resisting* the temptation to preach or correct the other person's viewpoint.
- Create a relational beachhead in a person's life. Who wouldn't want to talk again with someone who has shown herself to be a caring listener?
- Wear down a person's will to resist God. Free attention giveaways cause the recipient to trust you in spite of the fact that you are religious.

THE DAY SPA ORDINARY ATTEMPT

Darci, from Woodinville, Washington, has been following in the foot-
steps of Jesus and has mastered the art of asking great questions.

> I went downtown with my friend, and we treated each other
> to a facial.... I asked the gal who was slathering stuff on my
> face how she was doing and about her job, etc., and she said,
> "We really aren't supposed to tell about our sad lives to
> clients."
>   So I said, "Oh, go ahead. It helps to talk about your stuff.
> I process my stuff better when I get to talk about it."
>   She opened up and talked the whole hour about the sad-
> ness in her life: being separated, wanting kids and being thirty-
> four, feeling like she's in a dead-end job, feeling like she needed
> some spirituality in her life. I just listened and asked questions.
> After the facial, I left a tip in an envelope along with a note
> encouraging her to call out to God. "He digs it when we seek
> him and says we will find him if we seek him with all our
> hearts."

ATTEMPTING THE ORDINARY

This week, do something small for God. It can even be invisible—like listening carefully while someone tells you about his or her life. The only requirement is that you do it on purpose. None of us likes to be coerced, steered, or set up. All of us, however, regularly attempt to influence, redirect, guide, and even convert others to our point of view. If you're married or have kids, you know what I mean.

At Off The Map we refer to this spiritual practice as "nonmanipulative intentionality." It's fine to want your friend to know Jesus and to even attempt to persuade him or her to consider Jesus. But it's not fine to pressure, coerce, or steer your friend. Human beings don't like being manipulated, but we are receptive to influence.

Free attention giveaways allow you to influence your friend without manipulation. Following are two Ordinary Attempts, done on purpose but without manipulation, that you could try this week.

1. *The Phone Call Ordinary Attempt.* Denese, from Los Angeles, is a Christian who didn't want to lose touch with her missing friends. She is married, has two teenagers, and is active in her church. She knew that if she didn't do something on purpose, she would quickly lose contact with old friends, so she decided to set aside one hour every week to call her missing friends just to chat. She was amazed at how open and appreciative they were. She would tell them what she was up to spiritually if they asked, and they often did. Apparently, the phone provides a sense of protection that sometimes frees people to be more open and inquisitive.

Give this a try: Call a missing friend this week and ask her how she's doing. Do it on purpose, but don't steer the conversation. Restrain yourself from preaching. If your missing friend knows you're a Christian—and especially if you have attempted to "save" her in the past—she will be shocked that you didn't preach. It will stun her. She might even want to have coffee with you.

If the Phone Call Ordinary Attempt sounds a little too intense for you, try the Hold the Door for Someone Ordinary Attempt. It allows you to practice being intentional while protecting you from the risk of having to talk.

2. The Hold the Door for Someone Ordinary Attempt. Becky told me about a moment that made her day—or maybe it was bigger than that and made her year. She was a single mom with a young son and a full-time job. Dad was gone. Becky had just worked another long shift as a restaurant manager and was on her way home when she realized she needed gas. Stopping at a 7-Eleven, she was walking toward the main entrance when suddenly she became the recipient of an unsolicited act of relational kindness. Without warning an older man brushed past her, reached out, and opened the door for her. Becky was moved to tears by the kindness this man displayed.

Something so ordinary, so doable, as opening a door made a huge impact on Becky. Years later, now married, her children grown, and her life improved dramatically, Becky still remembers that small, ordinary act of kindness. It didn't cost the man anything to hold the door for Becky, and it didn't require any special knowledge or skill on his part. He held a door open for a stranger. Becky still cries when she tells the story.

CHAPTER 7

DO WHAT'S DOABLE

It's All You're Really Going to Do Anyway

Maybe you have a friend like Mike. Whenever I decide I'm ready to hear the unvarnished truth, I call Mike. He has the gift of pragmatism multiplied several times over. So if you don't want a reality check, don't call Mike.

During one of my many forays into establishing a regular exercise program, I asked Mike how many miles he thought I should run every day. He responded with a question: "What can you see yourself doing five years from now?"

I knew the answer, and it *wasn't* running. The only reason I considered running in the first place was to lose weight faster, not because I like to run. Running was a means to an end, not an end in itself.

The same is true when it comes to evangelism. We all need something we're passionate about, something we'll do because we're motivated from within, not just as a means to an end. We need to do what business leaders refer to as "getting better reality." When it comes to evangelism, what can you see yourself doing five years from now? Preaching on a street corner? Knocking randomly on doors all across your city? Approaching your friends with a memorized speech?

Dan Allender, president of Mars Hill Graduate School, explains how his school trains students in evangelism: "That's easy," he says, "we teach them how to order lunch."[1] Apparently, Dan believes that it *counts* when we have lunch with a friend and practice being unusually interested in him. That's doable for even the most introverted Christian among us. All Jesus asks of us is what's doable.

When Jesus decided to feed five thousand people, he asked his disciples to find enough food to take care of the situation. They, of course, knew that wouldn't be happening anytime soon. "In fact, all we've been able to dig up is this little kid's lunch. All told, it adds up to five loaves of bread and two measly fish." Jesus said that was great. He took what they did have instead of asking them to deliver what they couldn't possibly come up with. Jesus took one child's lunch and turned it into enough food to take care of thousands of hungry people.

When it comes to our nudging people along toward Jesus, all he needs from us is our ordinary life. To us it might look like a meager five loaves and two fish, but Jesus knows what we really have. He'll take what we do have over what we feel we *should* have any day. And then he'll make something beautiful out of it.

The Grocery Store Ordinary Attempt

I remember one of my very first Ordinary Attempts. This story is so unremarkable that if you have a traditional evangelist's bone in your body, you'll scoff at my experience. But here goes.

I was in the checkout line at the grocery store, and the clerk was a fast worker. I realized that I'd hardly have time to ask her how she was doing. Then I noticed she was wearing a button that said, "We want to adopt." I was surprised at her vulnerability, touched by her humility, and impressed with her boldness. This isn't something most people would readily advertise to hundreds of complete strangers.

As the other customers were dropping their items on the conveyor belt, I looked at the checker and said, "I have some friends who have adopted. I'll pray for you." She seemed genuinely touched that I noticed her. That was it. I wanted to let her know that God cared about her and was proud of her courage, vulnerability, and selflessness.

I didn't "share the gospel" with her, but I did share Jesus, the gospel creator. And I wasn't brave, bold, or smooth. I simply handed God the five loaves and two fish of my life and trusted him to turn them into something significant for that young woman. When God asks us to give him something, he asks us to give him only what we already have. It might take a little work to identify what that is, but we already have what we need to help move others closer to him. The problem is we don't think that what we have is enough.

One day Jesus took his class on a field trip to the temple, where they observed all sorts of people dropping money into the collection box. When a poor woman donated a penny, Jesus pointed out that from his perspective, she had given more than everyone else. (See Luke 21:1-4.) She gave more? More of what? Certainly, others had given a lot more money than this poor widow. By any measure, she gave less money than everyone else. What she gave was more heart, more authenticity, more honesty. She gave more of the currencies that attract God's attention. She gave more of what she had—rather than less of what she didn't have.

So often we do just the opposite. We try to give something we

don't have because we've been taught to believe that God pays attention to the big stuff. So we try to give more time, more money, more
bravery, and more effort, none of which we can sustain for any length
of time. We need to get better reality.

Value depends on scarcity and demand. The woman who gave
the penny captured Jesus's attention because she was giving herself
rather than a caricature of herself. Some of the evangelism practices
we have used force us to be something we aren't. We are asked to act
boldly, to be smart and quick on our feet. The woman who gave the
penny was being *real*, while the wealthy religious donors were being
fake. God wants us to be real even if it means that we have very little
to give. If it's real it gets his attention, because in God's economy, reality is scarce and in demand. That gives it tremendous value.

The Rule of 10 Percent

It turns out that all it takes to create a new product is making a 10
percent improvement on an old one. The trick of course is discover-
ing which 10 percent of the existing product or service needs to be
improved. That's where new ideas come from, and it explains why 80
percent of new ideas fail in the first year.

During the gas shortages of the 1970s, truck manufacturers were
looking for new ways to squeeze more mileage out of each gallon of
gas. Lots of big ideas flew at them, but they finally landed on making
a small design change to the nose of the truck. They rounded it about
10 percent, which had the immediate benefit of dramatically reduc-
ing fuel costs. The only problem with this change was one of perception. At the time all truck hoods were square. Truckers didn't feel like
real truckers when the noses of new trucks were rounded, but they

adjusted. Now rounded hoods are standard. A small design change eventually had big payoffs.[2]

Doing what's doable is a 10-percent change in the spiritual practice formerly known as evangelism, yet it has an amazing payoff. Some of the Ordinary Attempts described in this book may not look like evangelism to you. You may feel like the truck drivers who resisted the "sissy" redesign of their trucks. You may be thinking, *We need to drive* real *trucks like they used to make.* Or you might like the idea of doing what's doable, but wonder: *Is this* really *evangelism?*

Will simply doing what you're capable of doing, with no flash or polish or extra boldness, really enable you to lead someone into a heartfelt relationship with Jesus? It worked for a freedom fighter from Bhutan.

THE FREEDOM FIGHTER ORDINARY ATTEMPT

Rami comes from Bhutan, a small country north of India. Several years ago when he was a university student, Rami joined the Bhutanese freedom fighters. The government was corrupt, so students were taking their case to the streets. Rami was arrested, thrown in jail, and tortured. Eventually, his health broke and he was hospitalized. A Swedish nurse began caring for him, and without his permission, she began to pray behind his back. She never preached, but Rami figured out that she was a Christian.

A couple of years went by, and Rami was released from prison. He then received a letter from the nurse. She wrote that she would be happy to cover the costs of his university education. Rami accepted this generous offer and also anticipated a second letter from the nurse in which she would "preach" to him. But that letter never arrived. The nurse simply sent money. Rami, being a proud young man, decided that later on, when his beneficiary got around to making the tuition money contingent on his conversion to Christianity, he would quit school and pay back every penny.

Rami's friend never got around to preaching. More time passed, and Rami began wondering about life. He made friends with some Youth with a Mission workers who *did* preach. But by that time he was ready to hear the message. He decided to become a follower of Jesus. All of this was set in motion long before by a Swedish nurse who refused to do the expected and chose instead to do what was doable. She planted a seed. Years later someone else was there for the harvest. Rami's friend built an invisible bridge into his life without his even knowing it. The following story powerfully illustrates my point:

> During World War II, Russian soldiers at the Rzhev front, working at night in freezing waters, built a secret bridge under the river's surface. When darkness covered the moon and snow shrouded the river, strong Russian swimmers silently worked chest-deep in the freezing waters. Their bodies were bloodied by the ice floes.
>
> Then one morning, to the utter shock of the Nazis, Russian tanks, whitened for winter war, came charging down the bank, crashed through the thin ice, and stormed across the river on the hidden bridge built beneath the water. Squadron after squadron roared across toward the stupefied Nazis, opening the Rzhev offensive.[3]

A Swedish nurse built an invisible bridge to Rami, and much later Jesus used that bridge to cross into his life. The nurse did what was doable. She couldn't get Rami to listen to the gospel, but he was defenseless against experiencing the gospel through her generosity. Using a combination of free attention giveaways and kindness, she quietly constructed a bridge under the icy floe that separated Rami from God.

After talking with my friend Mike, the consummate pragmatist, I revised my exercise program. I gave up running and took up walking, something I knew I could still be doing in five years. That was ten years ago, and I've managed to stick with this exercise program, unlike some of my spectacular evangelism ideas.

ATTEMPTING THE ORDINARY

Jerry Seinfeld described his wildly popular television program as a "show about nothing." Week after week the writers drew upon the mundane practices of our ordinary lives and came up with another show about nothing. Seinfeld didn't invent a new idea (like the reality genre); instead, he and his crew celebrated ordinariness, which made all of us feel as if our ordinary lives counted.

Ordinary Attempts could also be called Seinfeld Evangelism. Basically, we make a big deal out of what some people think of as nothing. We count all the small, ordinary, and even mundane encounters in life. We look for Jesus in all the ordinariness the way Seinfeld looked for humor. We think it helps when, like Seinfeld, we make a big deal out of nothing.

Rami's nurse friend didn't think she was doing anything special; she was just doing what was doable. And if you give it some thought, you'll realize that you're already building a bridge to a missing person. It probably didn't occur to you sooner because you didn't think it counted. So this week, learn to celebrate doing what's doable. Tell someone about your bridge-building attempts. If you practice making a big deal out of small stuff, more and more surprises will come your way.

Go ahead: Make a big deal out of nothing. It counts in eternity.

CHAPTER 8

OUT OF RELIGION AND INTO REALITY

Dump the Religion Business

Unfortunately, Christianity got into the wrong business.

Like it or not, the church is competing today with soul providers and meaning makers like Oprah Winfrey, who appeals to her viewers' desire to "give back" through her Angel Network. We are in competition as well with *www.beliefnet.com,* which leads much of the online spiritual conversation that we could be leading. And we're mocked on numerous Web sites (often quite humorously) for the cartoonish practices and images we've successfully exported. We complain about cults using falsehoods to attract adherents, while we resort to false advertising, such as, "Accept Jesus and find happiness *all the time.*" We compare our best with their worst and hope they don't notice our inconsistencies. But they do!

Our critics do us a great service by pointing out our deficiencies.

We should take their advice and get out of the religion business. Jesus understood the religion business, and he had nothing good to say about it.

One day Jesus was asked to go to a Roman military officer's home to heal the man's servant. If it wasn't unusual enough for a Roman to invite a rabbi into his home, it gets even odder. The officer sent his friends to stop Jesus before he arrived at the house. The friends requested that Jesus "just say the word" (Matthew 8:8). The Roman officer didn't feel he was worthy of a personal visit from Jesus (see Luke 7:6-7). This spiritual outsider was demonstrating a kind of faith that apparently even Jesus hadn't seen before. Jesus turned to his followers and exclaimed, "I tell you the truth. I have not found *anyone* in Israel with such great faith." (Matthew 8:10).

This soldier, an enemy of Israel, may not have understood the Jewish religion, but he certainly had a clear grasp of reality. He needed real help real fast, and somehow he intuitively understood that Jesus was at the center of that reality. Jesus's endorsement of the centurion's insights into the new reality that Jesus was advocating astounded his listeners. The man he commended wasn't a Jew, and worse yet, he was part of the hated occupying army. How could a religious Jew side with a Roman centurion, a sworn enemy of Israel?

Simply put, Jesus wasn't in the religion business. He wasn't selling a religious point of view. His business was reality, and whenever he encountered a *reality seeker,* he responded to that person.

Here's what was so radical about Jesus's statement. He was calling his listeners to account, showing them they had somehow gotten into the wrong business. As a result, they didn't "get" why Jesus would say something as offensive as he did when he publicly endorsed this nonreligious guy's expression of faith. It's similar to the way we feel whenever Billy Graham prays with the "wrong" political leader (the one we disagree with).

Jesus could side with the religious outsider because faith is not the property of religion; it's the core of God's reality. People seeking this reality appear on God's radar whether they know it or not. And like the centurion, those people capture his attention. God begins trying to connect with the outsiders through us.

We need to dump the religion business and get back into a business we can excel at: the business of God's reality. Here's a story that shows what that looks like.

DEFENDERS OR PROCLAIMERS?

John Barce is a lawyer living in Fort Wayne, Indiana. He tries to follow the mission Jesus has given to all Christians—to connect with the people Jesus misses most in authentic, noncontrived ways. Perhaps because of this commitment, Barce unwittingly became embroiled in a controversial issue in his community. A group of Christians filed suit against a community college where a student wanted to produce a play that depicted Jesus as gay. The student was himself gay, and his planned theatrical production outraged many in the church community.

Barce read about the efforts to obtain a restraining order against the college to stop the play from being produced. Something about the legal action didn't sit right with him, so he decided to approach the student as a friend, not as a lawyer. He offered to deliver free pizza to the theatre troupe as they rehearsed for the play. He made himself available to serve this student and the cast. In so doing, Barce troubled many Christians who knew him. Why was he siding with the "enemy"? But in offering his friendship, Barce also intrigued his young friend.

Barce's question to the Christian community was this: What business are we in? Are we the defenders of God's reputation, or are we the proclaimers of his love? Does God need legal representation in our courts of law, or can he handle that in his own way? Does God need a public-relations agency to defend his honor when someone challenges it in such a public way, or is God secure enough in who he is that he can get by just fine without us rushing to his defense?

It is nowhere recorded in scripture that Jesus asked his followers to defend his reputation. While he was on earth, Jesus himself didn't bother correcting his critics. What people thought about him didn't seem to concern him that much. On the other hand, Jesus made the mission of proclaiming his love exceedingly clear. So John Barce decided to follow the mission that is presented plainly in scripture, and he befriended this student. The full impact of this friendship remains to be seen. As of this writing, the young man hasn't chosen to follow Jesus. But he did e-mail John Barce to say, "I only hope that when I'm given the opportunity in the future to serve someone who is different from me, I can do it with the same sensitivity and kindness you have shown me."[1]

Pretty real, huh? All John Barce did was deliver pizza and offer his friendship.

Now, think about this: Who has the greatest influence with this gay student—those wanting to correct or those trying to connect? Which is more important? Defending our moral rights or nudging someone closer to Jesus? You don't get to choose "both" as your answer. Which of the two is more important?

Who's Our Competition?

Southwest Airlines flies airplanes, but Southwest is not in the airline business. They're in the people-moving business. In the early days of Southwest, after the company began to show a small profit, some of the stockholders asked company president Herb Kelleher why he couldn't raise the ticket prices, since they were notoriously low. Kelleher responded, "You don't understand. We're not competing with other airlines; we're competing with ground transportation."[2]

Kelleher knew that in order for Southwest to get the attention of the traveling public, the airline would have to set its prices low enough to make people think twice about whether they should drive to their destinations. Of course, he still had to balance that with the actual costs of air transportation, but the vision was compelling. He even convinced his employees that Southwest wasn't in business but was in fact on a *crusade to set people free.* Southwest Airlines created the future by getting better reality about who the actual competition is. Interestingly, while some of the "big boys" of the airline industry have disappeared or are fighting bankruptcy, Southwest has maintained profitability.

When Jesus commended the Roman centurion's grasp of reality, it was like Southwest Airlines announcing a "Friends Fly Free" sale. Jesus lowered the bar to a place where even a hated Roman could enter the path of faith. This perturbed the religious, but it inspired the real to give God a try. God making himself accessible to mere mortals? Who wouldn't want to be in that business?

And think about this: When Jesus approached the centurion, he wasn't being *evangelistic;* he was simply being Jesus. When John Barce approached the gay student, he wasn't being *evangelistic;* he was just being John. They were being real. People don't need a better religion; they need a better reality. Let's dump religion and get back into the family business, the one we were born into—the reality business.

How to Get Real

When it comes to connecting with the people Jesus misses most, Christians need to risk, experiment, and get good at failing. We need to wonder about the possibilities we could explore, the adventures we could be part of, and the experiments we could attempt in partnership with Jesus. What if we started again from scratch, with no presuppositions?

What if…

- we gave people something *they wanted?*
- we could be *normal* around missing people?
- they *liked* us?
- they *told us* how we can help them connect with Jesus?
- we got rid of the fake caring, forced speeches, and slick tracts?

Sound like fun? Here are some ideas to help you get started:

1. Ask for help. When Levi Strauss jeans started lagging in sales several years ago, the president of the company decided to go to work as an undercover salesperson at a clothing store. He watched people pick up Levi's jeans, then put them down and buy jeans manufactured by one of his competitors. He asked people why they chose the other jeans over his, and armed with that information, he headed back to the executive suite and made changes that propelled his company to greater success. We need to learn from Levi Strauss and start asking for help.

I realized that I needed help, so I began interviewing a few people formerly known as "lost." Hannah and Jackie are two of the people I talked with. Here are some of the thoughts they shared about Christians. Listen as our customers explain why they aren't interested in our "spiritual jeans":

Jim: What does the term *born again* mean to you?

Hannah: The term *born again* conjures up the image of a very excited and overwhelmingly persistent, joyful, and talkative Christian.

Jim: Has anyone ever tried to get you "saved"?

Jackie: The only people who tried to "save" me were members of my own family and some people in my old church. It was really frustrating to have people I cared about and who cared about me not understand the decision I had made to not be a Christian and try to coerce me into going to church just "because." I always asked questions I needed answers to, but nobody gave me any legitimate answers. They just said I should go [to church] because it was the right thing to do.

Jim: Do you have any Christian friends?

Jackie: It has never been the case that I don't want to be friends with a Christian, but I have never had a Christian want to be friends with me.

Hannah: Many of my friends are Christian. Some go to church for the sake of forgiveness for the drinking

binge the week before; others have a close relationship with God, and I appreciate the strength of their
belief and faith in doing right. Although, of course,
they don't lead a much more "straight" path than
anyone else I know. My Muslim friends are actually
the most centered of any "religious" folk I know.

2. Attend AA meetings. If you want to see the most successful
grassroots spiritual movement in the world, attend an Alcoholics
Anonymous meeting and ask yourself, What can I learn from them
about connecting with my culture? AA has no visible leadership,
doesn't own a building, and will only accept a dollar from you. But
they know how to connect.

3. Hold an ignorance event. Invite someone who is an expert in
evangelism to speak to your church about his or her greatest evangelistic *failures.* It will do wonders for those listening and will inspire
them to go out and try failing themselves. Until failing is seen as simply another way to learn, we won't discover all the great ideas lying
just underneath the surface of our ordinary lives.

4. Create new categories. Who was the first person to fly the
Atlantic Ocean solo? Charles Lindbergh, right? Who was second?
Give up? His name was Bert Hinkler. Bert flew faster and used less
fuel than Lindbergh, but you don't know about him because he came
in second.

Who was the third person to fly solo across the Atlantic? Amelia
Earhart. Know why you know her? Not because she was third but
because she was the first woman to accomplish the task.

What we learn from Amelia is this: If you can't be first in a category, then create a new category to be first in. Or at least have fun
trying. Christians need to be more inventive and creative. Since the

majority of Christians can't compete with spectacular and dramatic evangelistic methods, we need to start practicing doable evangelism. This is a new category, created for the rest of us.

5. *Do your own video interviews.* Recently, my team and I went to Pike Place Market, a busy tourist spot in Seattle. We spent fifty dollars on ten Starbucks drink cards, and I held up a sign that said "Free Starbucks Card for Being Interviewed." When people asked, we explained that we were shooting video for a project on spirituality in culture.

We asked each person three questions:

- What is the difference between spirituality and religion?
- Who is a spiritual figure you admire?
- If Christians would listen to you, what would you say to them?

One woman said, "I would say that I am so grateful that I wasn't raised a Christian. They have such a limited worldview."

About half of the people (including "happy I'm not a Christian") asked us, "What are you guys doing?" For an investment of only fifty dollars and thirty minutes, we got people to *ask us* to tell them about our work for Jesus. We might even have changed a few minds about Christians.

Commit some money to paying people for their insights, but make sure you don't bait and switch them. Show the video at your church or to your leaders; they'll be surprised at how real it is.

6. *Don't forget to have fun.* Evangelism has become *way too serious.* We have managed to turn the very activity we should get so much joy out of into something we avoid. We need to recapture the fun and adventure of ordinary Christians doing ordinary things to nudge the people Jesus misses most across the starting line toward Jesus. We need to reclaim what I call *An Ordinary Christian's Bill of Rights:*

- You have the right to partner with God as he draws another person closer to himself.
- You have the right to speak on God's behalf and tell others about Jesus.
- You have the right to feel the beat of God's heart as someone begins to trust him.
- You have the right to watch God use your ordinariness to nudge people toward himself.

Call it sharing your faith, spreading the gospel, or serving God's kingdom. You can even call it evangelism if you want. The reason it won't go away is because it's one of the most dynamically spiritual activities we'll ever be involved in. We have a built-in desire to be part of the game. And it's a game for ordinary people like you and me.

ATTEMPTING THE ORDINARY

To refresh your memory on what it was like to be an evangelism target, go ahead and get lost for a day. You can get lost by trying one of the following. If you're *really* into it, try two or three of these ideas.

- Go to *www.off-the-map.org* and watch one of the interviews with three "lost" people. Use the video to spark a discussion with your small group, Sunday-school class, youth group, evangelism class, or spiritual community.
- Call several churches in your city and tell them you have a friend who is gay but is interested in attending church. Ask them what your friend might encounter at their church.
- Read the church advertisements in several newspapers. (You can check church ads from other parts of the country in Saturday papers at the local library.) Write down the terminology that is used to describe what these churches have to offer. Pay special attention to words that only Christians would understand. Photocopy some of the more interesting advertisements and ask a few non-Christian friends to tell you what they think of the ads.
- Photograph several church signs with a digital camera and show the photos to a few non-Christians. Ask them what they think the signs mean. Write down their responses and share them with your Christian friends.

If you try a few of these suggestions, you'll be reminded how odd the church and the Christian faith seem to those who aren't familiar with the jargon and the religious assumptions. You'll also realize what an "in-group" the church has become. And if you try the suggestions that involve getting input from your non-Christian friends, you'll also make your missing friends wonder about you in a good way. As a bonus, you will have taken a step toward becoming a more real human being—a step out of religion into reality.

CHAPTER 9

THE NEW HABIT OF BEING REAL

Get Better Reality

Colonial general Daniel Morgan had a problem. It was 1781, the British were coming, and his troops were losing their will to fight. These men had been sent as loaner troops from the northern states to assist the South Carolina militia. The only reason they didn't desert was because the Continental Army had a policy that if you ran you'd get a musket ball in the back.

The soldiers were outnumbered, out-trained, and outclassed by the crack British troops. General Morgan realized that "his militia could not be counted on to fight."[1] So he opted for an unorthodox battlefield maneuver. He instructed the militia *not* to hold their ground but instead to shoot two times and run. That's all. They only had to be brave for a short time; then they were free to run for their lives.

Morgan put the reluctant militia in the front lines and backed them up with more seasoned soldiers. As the British forces approached, the colonial soldiers did as instructed. They fired their guns two times and started retreating. But when they turned to look back at their pursuers, they discovered that the British troops were retreating. Emboldened by this turn of events, this ragtag bunch of undermotivated, very ordinary soldiers returned to the front line and began fighting *voluntarily.* They soon gained the advantage and soundly defeated the British.

Morgan's biggest opponent was not the superior British troops, but rather the fear within the minds of his own militia. To win the battle, he had to help them see that they had all the skills they needed. By asking these men to do *what they could do* and nothing more, General Morgan allowed them to choose when and where they would be brave.

When it comes to connecting with the people Jesus misses most, we don't have to be unusually brave. There's no pressure to do what we're not equipped to do and no shame in doing what we're well suited for. We only have to do what we can.

Praying Behind Their Backs

Sharon has three young children, and she cares deeply about connecting with the people Jesus misses most. She knew she wasn't going to go door-to-door to hand out evangelistic tracts, and she didn't feel confident about buttonholing people to listen to her testimony. Whatever she chose to do had to be simple and so doable that her kids could and would participate.

So Sharon started praying for other moms whenever she and her kids took a walk around a nearby lake. She would see other moms and their kids walking ahead of them, and she would talk to God about them. Sharon taught her kids that when they prayed for people, the Holy Spirit would actually do something to nudge those people closer to Jesus. By practicing strategic praying while she and her kids went for a walk, Sharon believed that Jesus would move those moms closer to God. She called it "praying behind their backs."

At this point, you might object: "Surely you're not counting walking around a lake and praying as evangelism!" Yes, in fact, I am counting it.

Is Sales Evangelism the Answer?

Let's say Sharon had taken the more traditional approach—what I call sales evangelism. She would have read a how-to book on evangelism, and after a few weeks of praying for boldness, she would have approached one of the moms walking around the lake. If her experience unfolded like many of ours have, it would have looked something like this:

Sharon introduces herself and asks the other mom what she
believes about God. (In sales evangelism you want the
"prospect" to feel a little off-balance so she doesn't have time
to bring up her objections.) The other mom gets wide-eyed
and answers Sharon's question with a curt response designed to
send the message that she doesn't want to continue the conversation. But Sharon isn't about to chicken out now, so she asks
the second question on the list she memorized from the evangelism book. The goal is to get the "information" delivered.

Sharon's stomach is in knots as she talks. It's clear the
other mom is becoming agitated. Sharon had not anticipated
that a few questions about God could elicit such a visceral
reaction. But she's been taught to ignore any "feelings" and to
just press on. Before Sharon can ask the third question, the
other woman hurries away, saying she has to get her kids
home for a nap.

So much for Sharon's initial experience with programmatic gospel sharing. Maybe it would get easier the next time.

Sharon didn't really do this. Like most of us, she's too chicken—
or maybe too real.

But the story is true nonetheless: Just change the name from
Sharon to Jim, or maybe to your own name. Many of us have tried
sales evangelism and achieved similar results. Since we've been inef-
fective with programmatic evangelism in the past, why do we still think
we can talk people into changing their minds about God? Before the
days of telephone no-call lists, we hated to pick up the phone during
dinner only to have a stranger try to sell us new windows or give us a
quote on auto insurance. Telemarketers operated on the principle that
if they just kept talking, we'd roll over and hand them our check-
books. Those subscribing to the sales evangelism model aren't dramatically different. They believe if they just keep talking, they'll
eventually talk *someone* into changing his mind and accepting Christ
as his personal Savior.

It's time to get real. It's time to consider an alternative. Most of us
hate the artificial, confrontational tactics of sales evangelism, much as
General Morgan's reluctant soldiers hated facing the highly trained
British troops. But what is it that we *are* willing to do? Are we brave

enough to take the step of praying for people behind their backs? Are we brave enough to believe that Jesus will honor our prayers for the people he misses most? Like General Morgan's soldiers, we already know how *not* to be brave. But a funny thing happens when we realize that we don't *have* to be brave. Like Morgan's reluctant soldiers, we often *choose* to be brave.

BE A COWARD FOR JESUS

As I was walking out of a Christian bookstore one day, a title caught my eye: *Conspiracy of Kindness.* I immediately knew that it was a book about evangelism written from a completely new point of view. I consumed the book and attended a conference, where I met the author, Steve Sjogren.[2]

Steve introduced me to new ways of practicing and thinking about evangelism that were real and fun. His innovation and generosity have had a major influence on my life. He started a club called CFJ, Cowards for Jesus. This is a group of Christians who desperately *want* to be brave for Jesus but are more like Woody Allen than Mel Gibson. I am the poster child for Cowards for Jesus.

I'm convinced that most Christians are closet members of CFJ and are suffering from a malady called EFD, evangelism frustration disorder. This occurs when Christians insist on trying to be something they're not—namely, brave.

Jesus didn't ask us to be brave (most of the time); he asked us to be ourselves. That means we are ordinary, normal, dysfunctional human beings who know we are loved by Jesus. When we manage to communicate that message to our missing friends, they think it sounds like good news.

If you're a coward for Jesus, you win without fighting. It's common knowledge among great generals that frontal assaults are rarely effective, so instead, they try to go around or leapfrog their opponents whenever possible.

One advantage CFJers bring to the task of connecting with the people Jesus misses most is that we are *predisposed to wanting to go around them*. We don't naturally take the lead in a frontal assault. We aren't going to have a sudden personality change that moves us to enlist as a "marine for Jesus." We are the evangelistic equivalent of the kid with five loaves and two fish. Our lives are more like a *Seinfeld* episode than an episode on *Survivor* in which we're the last person standing. How Jesus uses our small contribution seems more coincidental than intentional. And that's fine with us.

SURPRISE AND MYSTIFY PEOPLE WITH KINDNESS

Not long after Sharon included her children in praying for people behind their backs, she tried something entirely different during the busy Christmas shopping season. Here's how Sharon tells it:

> I was standing at the checkout counter in a toy shop, and I overheard one of the salesgirls (a college student) telling one of the other salesgirls that she was exhausted, hungry, and needed a break. But all she had was $3.25, which wasn't quite enough to get the deli sandwich she really wanted.
>
> The other gal said, "Why don't you just buy a bagel?" The first girl said she could, but she was really craving a deli sandwich. So I reached over the counter, handed her a five dollar bill, and said, "Merry Christmas!" She took the money, started

to cry, and came around the counter and hugged me. Two other salesgirls stood there looking perplexed, along with a number of customers.

I then handed each of the salesgirls a coupon for a free beverage at Starbucks and said, "Merry Christmas." They accepted the coupons and continued to stare at me. I then asked if I could pay for the toys I was buying. They looked kind of flustered and started to ring the items up.

One of the gals asked me, "Why did you do this?" I said, "Because Jesus loves you, and Christmas is all about him giving his life for you." They stood there looking very perplexed, finished ringing me up, and said thank you. It was so much fun!

Sharon decided when and where she would be brave. She prayed behind people's backs for a long time and then while Christmas shopping, she practiced another way of being real by sharing the generosity of Jesus with a tired, hungry store clerk.

Sociologists tell us that we tend to repeat what we enjoy. We voluntarily put our hearts and souls into doing the things that delight us. If it's fun and fulfilling, Christians will gravitate toward an approach that feels more like real life and less like a sales pitch. Sharon wasn't evangelizing; she was simply being herself. And an overworked college student, trying to make some extra money during Christmas break, got a deli sandwich from a customer who kindly shared the joy of the season. Everyone was a winner.

Jesus gave us a mission, and he doesn't require experts to get the job done. There is no B team when it comes to whom he'll use. A willingness to be real, a willingness to give away attention by praying for those Jesus misses most, a willingness to be ourselves around the missing—these simple spiritual practices qualify us to be part of the mission of Jesus.

LESSONS IN BEING REAL

Being real means being yourself without being weird or obnoxious. It means bringing your Jesus Story into the room with you if it's called for, and it means that if God prompts you to do something overtly spiritual, you go for it. A woman who practices Ordinary Attempts tells about a time she hesitated to pray for her daughter and her daughter's roommate. But God nudged her, so she moved forward and pointed them toward Jesus.

> My twenty-one-year-old daughter has a friend who…has visited church, and while she doesn't actively explore [spiritual things], there are times when I sense the Holy Spirit is pursuing her and she seems open to faith. She was over with my daughter last night. The two of them had been house hunting for days. They came in to tell me about a house they found that they really liked and wanted to rent.
>
> I sensed the Holy Spirit challenging me to offer to pray for them. I actually had a small conversation with the Holy Spirit (in my mind), telling him that if I put him on the line like that and they didn't get the house, it would not be a good thing. He said he could handle that, so I asked them if they wanted me to pray. My daughter said no, but her friend immediately said yes. My daughter said to her friend, "You don't even believe in God," and her friend said, "Yes I do. I'm just not sure what I believe."

So I asked my three-year-old-son, Alex, to pray with me and ask Jesus to help them get the house. I led him in the prayer, and we prayed that God would show them that he was paying attention to their needs and that he would give them favor with the landlord.

I just got a call from my daughter and her friend saying that the landlord called them today.... He said he had a good feeling about them, and they could have the house.... My daughter's friend thanked me because she believed that God answered my (and Alex's) prayer and gave them favor.

Jesus gave us a mission, and that mission is to connect in real ways with the people he misses. Start practicing the new habit of being real, and you'll start having more fun and experiencing connections with missing people that are more real.

ATTEMPTING THE ORDINARY

Get real by practicing being your nonreligious self (a.k.a. "the real you"). Many of us are confused about how to be intentional in our ministry to the missing without being manipulative. We struggle to differentiate between intentionality and manipulation. How can we learn to suggest without steering and to engage without controlling? How do we go about building trust with someone whose eternal future or present life we seek to influence?

We call this practice "nonmanipulative intentionality." Following is a list of questions that are spiritual but not overtly Christian. They will help you practice how to be your spiritual self (the real you) and avoid trying to be your artificial, "religious" self. Practice using these questions with your missing friends this week and notice what happens to you and maybe even to them.

- What are *your* spiritual interests?
- What do you think of Christians?
- What do you think of Jesus?
- Would you pray for me (yes, me)?
- What would you like prayer for?

Ask lots of questions; people have lots of opinions. And as you ask, resist the urge to spiritually fix them.

CHAPTER 10

HAVE YOU LUSTED LATELY?

Good Intentions Count Too

Why, according to many bible teachers, do we earn demerits for lusting but receive no rewards for listening? Is it really true that bad intentions get God's attention, but good ones don't?

In the gospel of Matthew, Jesus provided a hidden-camera view into God's heart with his comments regarding the final judgment: "Come, you who are blessed by my Father; take your inheritance.... Whatever you did for one of the least of these [prisoners, orphans, and those who are hungry]...you did for me" (Matthew 25:34,40). Jesus made it clear that it really does count to him when people anonymously care for other human beings. Jesus notices it even if the people who are doing these things don't. Seemingly unremarkable and very ordinary attempts to love others really do get Jesus's attention.

I'm not suggesting that we earn our way into heaven by doing good things. But to say that our good deeds don't get God's attention would be to deny a common-sense reading of Jesus's statement. Those Jesus rewards aren't keeping track of their acts of kindness, but apparently Jesus is. They aren't looking to score points, but he rewards them anyway.

It's interesting to note that the religious folks of Jesus's day—those who were trying hard to earn extra points—actually missed the point. They were doing the right external things, but Jesus doesn't count the externals; he counts the invisible. He examines the internal motives and intentions of the heart. Those who were loving others out of their love for Jesus got his attention, while those who did all the right things but for the wrong reasons got problems.

This is what Jesus meant when he said, "If anyone gives even a cup of cold water to one of these little ones because he is my disciple...he will certainly not lose his reward" (Matthew 10:42). The words "if...because" are the key. They express the practice of non-manipulative intentionality. It tells us that actions that engage others without trying to control them, and of goodness and kindness that serve others without trying to steer them, all *count* to Jesus. These practices really do get his attention.

Jesus's statement in Matthew 25 regarding "the least of these" correlates wonderfully with his analogy of giving a cup of water to a little child (see Matthew 10:42). Children often don't recognize or even appreciate our acts of kindness, but they still benefit from these acts. The same is true when we serve the people Jesus misses most. The time we spend with them and the attention we pay them may or may not register in their mind as intentional kindness, but it always registers with Jesus, and he rewards us.

What's our reward? When I sense that one of my missing friends now trusts me or when that person initiates a conversation with me about life or Jesus, I feel as if I just won the lottery. That's my reward.

To the God who counts what's invisible, our kind intentions look just like the five loaves and two fish a little boy gave him two thousand years ago. It's all he needs to set up a feast of creative circumstances in a person's life as he nudges that person further along the path toward himself. Bottom line: When we're loving people by listening to them or being unusually interested in their story, Jesus gets it! He really does use these ordinary things.

Several years ago, when I was pastor of a church in Seattle, I used a Burgermaster fast-food joint as my personal corporate center for strategic studies. Translation: I went there each week to put my sermons together. My booth, with books and papers in various piles, stood out as an oddity amid the local lunch crowd. Bob, the owner, would stop by and ask what I was up to. I told him I was trying to put together a talk about God. Over time I started asking his opinions about spiritual topics. And eventually I began using some of his ideas in my talks.

Burgermaster Bob was shocked. Not only was I intentionally listening to him (we talked weekly), but I also valued his thoughts. This went on for a few years. I didn't do it just for the fun of it (although it *was* fun); I did it on purpose to try to connect with Bob and nudge him closer to Jesus.

I recently ran into Bob, and we caught up on the past two years. I asked him about his business, and he kindly asked about my "church" work. While we were talking I remembered that he had once told me about his wife studying a New Age kind of spirituality with the hope of becoming a teacher. It was a natural transition, so I inquired about her current level of interest.

"Oh, she decided that telling other people how to live their lives wasn't for her," Bob told me. I asked if he and his wife would be willing to take a look at my Web site, and I mentioned that I'm in a group that uses some of my wife's writing to spark discussion on spirituality. He said they would take a look at her work on the Web site and let me know what they thought. That was my reward! Jesus was telling me that he was happy about this connection with Bob and that he was taking care of things.

Does this count as evangelism? Absolutely! I simply suggested that Burgermaster Bob and his wife check out my decidedly non-New-Agey Web site and give me their feedback.

For a long time Bob and I had been real with each other, and we had earned each other's trust, which brought our relationship to this point. When we love people, Jesus gets involved! And *we* get the reward of being trusted and befriended by those Jesus misses most. A small offering of our time, our kindness, or our attention shown toward others is all Jesus needs to set up a series of divine coincidences in people's lives as he nudges them further along the path toward himself.

SHOW ME THE MONEY

When my wife and I lived in India, getting our money exchanged was a big event. Once we got to the office of the local money exchanger, he would take our American dollars and carefully count them in a back room. Then he'd return and, it seemed to me, count out our rupees very quickly. I had to pay close attention to make sure that he and I were counting the same way.

Likewise, the way we count things and the way God counts

things is often very different. Humans count the visible stuff—things we can see, hear, and feel—while God keeps accurate tabs on the things that are much harder to count. Things like a smile, a hug, or the sacrifice of time.

I finally got the hang of counting with the money-exchange guy in India. Similarly, learning to "see" and count the invisible things that God values is a skill we can acquire with practice. Will we continue to count only the "big" or visible things, or could we learn to count the invisible things as well?

Until a very sensitive scale was invented, a lot of gold dust went the way of all flesh—dust to dust. Without a measure, there is no treasure. Many people who could have become rich walked right past their treasure. They recognized value only in the nuggets. They couldn't see value in the dust, the barely visible specks of gold.

The Christian community shares a similar faulty measure. Most pastors have learned to count the seated rather than the served—we call it church growth. This way of measuring can be a cruel taskmaster. Every Sunday we get out the clicker to tally up the score. A few superstar churches feel good about their results, but the majority of us wonder if we should even bother showing up for next weekend's game.

THE WHISPERING PINES ORDINARY ATTEMPT

Here's how one church learned to count the served instead of the seated. A few years ago some friends were praying for an outreach strategy in the community that surrounds their church in Seattle. During a prayer meeting they felt impressed to serve a low-income apartment complex called Whispering Pines.

The complex is operated by the county housing authority. Our leadership team agreed to take this project on for a year. We would do outreaches around Thanksgiving, Christmas, and whenever else we could.

We approached the housing-authority management in October and asked if we could give away Thanksgiving dinners. We raised enough money to give away thirty baskets of food and asked the management if we could deliver the baskets to the families in greatest need. They welcomed our efforts, but with two conditions: (1) We could deliver the baskets as long as a housing-authority staff person went with us; and (2) we had to agree not to mention that we were from a church unless a recipient asked.

To say the least, this was disappointing. We wanted people to *know* why we were giving away groceries—to show God's love in a practical way. However, we decided that God had directed us, so we agreed to the conditions. We prayed over the event and delivered the food baskets without seeing anything big happen. (By the way, a couple of church people asked if we could sneak cards into the baskets, saying, "This was brought to you by our church because it's our way of showing God's love." But we resisted this suggestion and respected the management's conditions.)

Then, as Christmas drew near, the apartment managers called and asked if we would help with the annual Christmas party they put on for the residents. We volunteered to provide a Santa, gifts for children, crafts, and caroling. Again, we weren't able to mention that we were from a church unless someone asked.

After Christmas we received a thank-you note from the housing authority. They later agreed to our request to do an Easter-egg hunt the day before Easter. They even asked us to write an article in their monthly newsletter, and they produced fliers advertising the hunt. On all the printed material, they added the name of our church as the sponsor of the event. We had a breakthrough!

For Easter we had an Easter bunny, an egg hunt, and food baskets with ham dinners and gift certificates for groceries for all thirty-five families in the apartment complex.

The following month the associate executive director for the housing authority called to ask if we could meet for coffee. While we visited she and another woman from her organization told us they were impressed with our efforts to serve this community. Plus, because we didn't force God on the residents, we were now welcome to do whatever we wanted to do in the future, including outreaches and bible studies.

Following that conversation we held a back-to-school barbecue with games, and we gave away school supplies. By the way, the housing authority sent some people to observe the barbecue to see how our faith community interacted with the residents. They weren't spying on us; they were using us as an example of how faith-based communities and the county social services can work together.

The following Thanksgiving we gave away fifty food baskets and helped serve at the residents' community Thanksgiving dinner. After that we organized a Christmas party and passed out invitations to the residents with RSVP cards for the kids, asking their age, gender, etc. We were able to buy appropriate gifts for ninety kids! It was an awesome time.

God has opened up so much opportunity that we can't keep up, and when we launched this straightforward act of kindness, we never even mentioned his name to those who received food baskets. We had to start out just by being his hands and feet.

As it turned out, we never did a Vacation Bible School or a gospel outreach, but something better happened. When our church relocated recently, another church that was inspired by our efforts adopted Whispering Pines. And because of the great relationship we had earned with the housing authority, they have asked us (*begged* would be more accurate) to take on an after-school tutoring program for ninety-three kids at another low-income apartment complex closer to our new location. We're certain that we'll get time with these kids to talk about Jesus. That is what counts to us.

Go and Communicate the Gospel

As I mentioned earlier, communication experts tell us that the truly important elements of any message sent between two people are eye contact, tone of voice, and body language. Effective communication can be reduced to this: Show me; don't tell me.

If this is true, then when we are practicing free attention give-aways, we really are *preaching*. The Christians who volunteered at the Whispering Pines apartment complex didn't mention God unless they were asked, but their preaching was getting through loud and clear.

Do actions count as evangelism? I would argue that they do. God sees differently than we do. He notices the subtleties of life—our intentions, our caring, and our willingness to listen and learn from others. He *sees the invisible* and counts it.

In the fascinating book *Zero: The Biography of a Dangerous Idea,* Charles Seife explains that at one time the number zero was considered dangerous. "The Greeks so despised zero that they refused to admit it into their writings, even though they knew it existed." Why? "Zero clashed with one of the central tenets of Greek philosophy...there is no void."[1]

The only cultures that allowed zero were the Arabs and East Indians. The Greeks and those influenced by Greek thinking, including the church, rejected this "invisible" number because allowing it into their thinking would imply that infinity existed and that the universe was not a closed system and, by extension, controllable and knowable. "Within zero there is the power to shatter the framework of logic," Seife notes.[2] Consequently, the Greeks blocked its use in the West for more than two thousand years, with the church's support, until eventually the need for technology to develop better military weapons forced its acceptance.

Similarly, the Pharisees found Jesus's invisible counting system intolerable. He would take small things, ordinary people, and unspectacular events, such as having dinner with someone or spending a few minutes with a woman who interrupted him on his way to heal a young child, and turn them into his primary teaching moments. He was constantly using these moments of ordinariness rather than the more popular images of power.

We live in a world of numbers—credit-card numbers, pounds lost or gained, cell-phone minutes, Internet passwords. But counting involves more than numbers. We count what matters most to us and *discount* that which doesn't. Why all this talk about counting and what counts to God? Here's why: If something doesn't count to you, you won't keep doing it. Jesus said that "where your treasure is, there your heart will be also" (Matthew 6:21). What we treasure determines where we put our heart. If something doesn't "count" to me, if I don't value or treasure it, my heart won't be connected to it. That's why we need to practice God's math and learn to count the invisible, the small, and the ordinary.

To God, it counts when you listen while your co-worker pours out her heart to you over a cup of coffee. It counts when you smile at someone or ask the waitress at lunch about her life outside of work. It even counts when you pray behind someone's back.

When we do these invisible things, God notices. He sees you nudging your friend slowly, gradually across the starting line toward Jesus. God sees your heart. And he will reward you with more and more connections with the people he misses most.

ATTEMPTING THE ORDINARY

For the next seven days, pray Penny Prayers. Whenever you find a penny, pick it up, and as you do, pray a short prayer for the missing person of your choice. Name the person and ask God to bring him or her into his kingdom. Don't save the pennies; just notice how many you find in a week. Ignore dimes and quarters.

When you notice a penny on the ground and bend down to pick it up and pray for a specific person, you are turning your attention and your heart toward that person. As you ask God to draw that person closer to his heart, your own heart is becoming more sensitive toward those Jesus misses most. You're becoming more real.

Note: Continue to practice Penny Prayers while you think of a more "spiritual" way to remember to pray for people.

CHAPTER 11

WHO'S LOST—US OR THEM?

They Can't Locate God; We Can't Locate Them

O ver the past few years, people from all over the world have sent in hundreds of stories describing how they have found a more natural way to connect with their not-yet-Christian friends. Out of all this, a ministry came about that we call Off The Map.

When we do events, the most highly anticipated segment is The Interview with Three Lost People. We do this live. (You can watch these interviews at *www.off-the-map.org.*) Three non-Christians come onstage in front of hundreds of pastors. I start the interview with the Off The Map Pledge of Kindness, during which the people in the audience commit to *not preach* at our guests.

People have asked how I manage to motivate three people we call "lost" to come onstage to discuss why they never plan on becoming Christians. (Imagine how you'd feel if you were invited to address a conference for terrorists and were asked to speak about "Why I never want to be like you.") Here's how I get non-Christians to do this: I really do like missing people, and they are surprised to find that a Christian is genuinely interested in their opinions. Together, the guests and I use these interviews to intrigue and provoke the audience toward a new way of thinking about the people Jesus misses most.

During the interviews the guests tell us what Christians look like from their perspective and offer tips on how we can improve. Our tag line is "Those who aren't born again talk back to those who are."

Here are a few insights gleaned from the interviews:

Q: If Christians weren't pushy, would you be willing to be friends with one?

A: I have had numerous encounters with representatives of Christian groups on college campuses who have tried to get me to come to their groups and have asked me questions about my beliefs. They bring up all those old feelings I have about being a bad person for my decision not to be a Christian. And to be honest, they scare me. I'm always afraid to say what I really want to say around them, and how can you be someone's friend if you don't tell the truth? I do, however, have three friends who are Mormons, and in some respects they are pushy too, and I am afraid of offending them. But we all learned to disregard matters of faith and just be friends with each other.

Q: Tell me about your church experiences as a young person.

A: I actively disliked every youth-group activity I went to, even though I remember trying to have a positive attitude about it all. I remember feeling like *important* things just weren't talked about in church—like everyone wanted to skate over all the questions I had. (I was still struggling with the Jesus question, big time, among all the other typical things: What happens to people of other religions? Why would God let evil happen? Why won't God forgive Satan?) So I guess I just put it all down and began looking for my own answers, far outside of what church was telling me.

Q: When did you first encounter a born-again person?

A: I have never met a born-again Christian. I have met two ex-born-againers, and I have an acquaintance from high school who has since become a born-again, but I've never met one face to face. I met an obnoxious preacher who used to come to campus, though. He screamed at people about going to hell and fornicating and being gay and stuff. I used to look forward to his visits, actually, because I thought it was really funny. I mean, it really was—just completely bizarre and utterly ridiculous. I remember thinking, *Man, this guy needs to take some classes or something.* I've never heard of a good salesman operating that way.

Terrorist Evangelism

If evangelism-by-frontal-assault works, then let's all start carrying large signs that say, "You are lost. You are bad. You are an idiot! Ask *me* for help!" Like it or not, that's often how we appear in the eyes of the people Jesus misses most.

The people formerly known as lost often already know they're in trouble. They know they need help. The problem is that, just like us, they're not anxious to broadcast their inadequacy. That's why they react negatively to our frontal assaults—not necessarily because they disagree but because they are too proud to openly admit their vulnerabilities. How about you? Do you find it easy to admit you're wrong? You've got Jesus, and I'll bet you still find it challenging to humble yourself. Why do we expect that getting missing people to admit their need should be easy or simple?

SNOOPING IN THE BLOGOSPHERE

Blogs are a fascinating way to eavesdrop on people. Bloggers write down their innermost thoughts knowing and *hoping* that complete strangers will read them. I snoop blogs looking for conversations about evangelism. Here's one from a pastor in Canada in which he talks about turning terrorist evangelism into an opportunity to connect with the people Jesus misses most.

> I...found myself at Tim Horton's [a restaurant]. I sat watching two people "tag-team evangelize" a young couple.... It seemed to me that every move was designed to put pressure on the couple to realize that Jee-sus was the best way, the only way, the right way, etc.
>
> I found myself getting angrier and angrier. So I took a deep breath—and intervened. I put a stop to the bashing that was going on. I had a wonderful discussion with the evangelists, taking the heat off the couple. After leaving their tracts with me and the couple, they headed out to continue their ministry.

I spent some time talking with the couple. They were angry. They felt browbeaten. They felt threatened. One of them said, "It's no wonder that Christianity is a dying religion, with crap like that." We talked for nearly an hour about a whole bunch of things—including the faith stances of these two people. We talked about where their faith understandings fit with what [the] "tag team" had been saying, and where they didn't. [The couple] talked about their understandings of God, of Christ, of Spirit. We talked about creeds and faith statements and living faith....

Strange; they easily fit within my understanding of followers of Christ.

It was interesting. I could see in their faces that they were a bit shocked when, as we were getting ready to go on with our morning, one of them asked me what I did for a living. When I explained that I'm a minister, one of the two said, "Would you mind if we checked out some of the things happening at your church?"[1]

Who Isn't Lost?

Brian McLaren believes that *both* the missing and the church have lost their way. Those who are missing are unsure how to locate God, and the church seems unsure about how to find the missing. We have majored in the minors and failed to become expert in our primary task—connecting with the people Jesus misses most. We're both lost.

At each Off The Map conference, we set up The Wailing Wall of Flawed Evangelism Attempts. Over the course of two days, attendees make their way to the wall to write down some evangelistic memory they'd just as soon forget.

Here are some confessions we found on the wall:

Some Christian friends and I surrounded a guy at school and told him God wanted him to come to an evangelistic meeting. He came and "prayed the prayer" but was so freaked out that whenever he saw me from then on, he would literally turn and run. I'm sorry.

1983–1988 were what I now think of as my "pious years." During that time I told my Mormon sister as well as many street people that they would go to hell. I never saw one conversion. I'm sorry, Lord.

I slipped and got high with a guy I was trying to witness to, only to have him call me a hypocrite. Please send your word to him now.

In an attempt to be open with a girl I was interviewing for a job, I asked several questions about her life. She described her very recent wedding that took place in a forest. "Cool," I said. "What's your husband's name?" "Jill," she replied. My mouth dropped down so far, I think it hit my knees. I blew it and didn't know how to continue.

I once asked a teenage girl to "pray the prayer" while her mother was present. The mom objected. I prayed with her anyway. God, please forgive my abuse.

A group of us were going to go witness at a psychic fair after church. We met before church in a room adjacent to the sanctuary and proceeded to get in a big fight about how we were going to approach this project. The fight continued right through the service, and our yelling got so loud that the pastor had to send someone in to quiet us down. Needless to say, our trip ended up a disaster. (Yes, we still went out and totally blew it.)

How do you feel when you read these comments? It appears as if we've been trained to care about the "lost" just as long as they are moving toward our goal for them. But if we detect a deviation in their direction, we change our behavior, communicate disapproval, and often drop them from our list. We only *pretend* to like them. How did we acquire that kind of artificiality?

TWO CONVERSIONS

In Acts 10, we find the story of Cornelius and Peter. Cornelius was part of the outsider group as far as Peter was concerned. Even though Peter was a leading follower of Jesus, he still had not completely let go of the old paradigm. It could be argued that Cornelius could have been converted to Christ without Peter being present. But it's doubtful that Peter would have been converted *again* to Jesus had he not made the trip.

Prior to his encounter with Cornelius, Peter had a decidedly "Jewish for Jesus" bias. He had been told explicitly and repeatedly by Jesus to go into *all* the world. Jesus spelled it out with even greater specificity in his very last words when he told Peter (and the other apostles) again to go into Jerusalem, Judea, Samaria, and the utter-most parts of the earth (see Acts 1:8). Nevertheless, Peter remained in Jerusalem, and only under pressure did he travel to Samaria to put his stamp of approval on the outpouring of the Holy Spirit. Then once again he headed back to Jerusalem!

Fortunately for Peter (and the rest of us), none of this dissuaded Jesus from once again trying to get through to him. Finally, in Acts 10, Jesus opened up *The Picture Bible* to Peter and patiently explained the plan one more time. Peter met up with Cornelius and, as we say, "the rest is history." As a result of this meeting, not only was Cornelius converted; Peter himself experienced another conversion into Jesus.

Each time I interview a missing person, I experience a deeply personal conversion—mine, not theirs. I get touched. I see the kingdom of God in a new light. I feel Jesus loving these people through me and hopefully giving them a brief glimpse of his heart. For me those moments are like heaven on earth. They are all the reward I'll ever need.

How Jesus Practiced Evangelism

Many of us have been trained to orient our bible reading around the miracle stories of Jesus. The healings, the multiplication of food, the walking on water, the calming of the wind and sea, the casting out of demons. For some people, these stories are allegorical; for others they are literal and instructional. Regardless of your interpretation, I want to ask you an honest question: When was the last time you personally participated in anything remotely similar to these miraculous events?

I've spent a significant portion of my Christian life and ministry pursuing the transrational works of Jesus. I have personally prayed for healing for the sick, and I have cast out demons. Most Christians I've talked with have never attempted these practices, at least not consistently. It's hard work, but it's very rewarding when the results come. I have immense admiration for Christians who have dedicated their lives to pursuing the miracles of Jesus. But the simple fact is that for most of us, these experiences are irregular and inconsistent at best. The majority of Christians I know rarely experience the miraculous.

If anyone could have used extraordinary means to evangelize the "lost," it was Jesus. The Son of God could have called down lightning and fireballs and hosts of angels as a testimony to God's greatness and the neediness of humankind. But he didn't. *At least not to the extent or with the frequency that he could have.* He could have set up shop in the temple and held a healing crusade that *always worked* day in and day out for three-and-a-half years. He could have offered a simple contract and delivered on it consistently: "If I heal you (or, more accurately, *when* I heal you), will you agree to accept me as your personal Lord and Savior and follow me for the rest of your life?" Think how effective that would have been. People had no health-care plan, and they had limited amounts of food. Who in their right mind would have said no to such an offer?

I wish he had done this. I wish I could do it. But he didn't, and I can't. I'm stuck following the Jesus who hid himself as an ordinary fisherman, gardener, and short-order cook. I'm stuck following the Jesus who, while functioning in a league above us mere mortals, nevertheless displayed some reassuring traits of ordinariness and humanity, such as the inability to always control his circumstances, not always getting his own way, moments of not completely understanding what was going on (think of his questions in the Garden of Gethsemane), and admitting his vulnerability to his three closest disciples. This is why I follow Jesus. I still pray for the miraculous, but I no longer devote my best energy to that. I spend my time now trying to "see" Jesus in the ordinary. It is in the ordinary that I feel drawn to be more like him.

THE ORDINARY IN THE MIRACLE

Jesus performed miracles, but he did it in the context of ordinary life. It is in this interplay that we discover his approach to moving people toward change regardless of their spiritual status. Here is a story from what I call Jesus's Mission to the Missing:

> A ruler came and knelt before him and said, "My daughter has just died. But come and put your hand on her, and she will live." Jesus got up and went with him, and so did his disciples. (Matthew 9:18-19)

Missing people come in all shapes, sizes, and stations in life. Jesus heals the poor, saves the rich, and responds to the religious. No sooner does he befriend one group than he turns around and connects with their sworn enemies. He just can't be tamed.

The ruler of the synagogue, a decidedly religious man, was so despondent over his daughter's death that he abased himself at the feet of the leader of this radical sect of Nazarenes. Ever been there? Without saying a word, Jesus headed for the man's house, no doubt leaving his disciples scratching their yarmulkes and trying to make sense out of yet another Jesus moment. "I thought this was one of the guys Jesus called 'snakes,'" they likely murmured. "Now he's heading off to resuscitate one of their kids. What's up with that?"

When you pursue the missing, you intentionally betray the opinions of the culture you come from. You do so in order to invite those who are willing to walk the narrow tightrope of love away from the broad (and dangerous) path that leads to lifeless living.

Jesus Misses Women Too

> Just then a woman who had been subject to bleeding for
> twelve years came up behind him and touched the edge of
> his cloak. She said to herself, "If I only touch his cloak, I will
> be healed." (Matthew 9:20-21)

Jesus was heading to the religious ruler's home. And just when the ruler was feeling hopeful that Jesus would do something about his daughter who had died, Jesus got stopped by a woman. The gender of the person who interrupted their progress doesn't strike us as important, but when it's read in the context of first-century Palestine, this moment is filled with cultural complexity.

If you picture it like a scene out of a movie, you can appreciate the complex levels of communication taking place. Stage left you have the already confused disciples. Now picture the spiritually tentative religious leader who is trying desperately to maintain a very fragile grasp on faith in the power and ability of this radical Rabbi. Just then, from the opposite corner appears a woman who is slowly bleeding to death. This woman's cultural value is just a short notch above a leper, and she is brash enough to interrupt all these busy and powerful *men*.

Jesus stops.

Missing people present themselves to us in uneven and unplanned ways. They are just like us—they have *very* personal problems.

So Christians who are on a mission to the missing get good at stopping, noticing, and listening.

> Jesus turned and saw her. "Take heart, daughter," he said,
> "your faith has healed you." And the woman was healed from
> that moment. (Matthew 9:22)

Jesus read the woman's heart. He felt her faith, her need, and her trust. He *announced* healing. Nothing else is recorded. He didn't ask her to commit to anything or to change anything. He just gave to her.

The art of connecting could also be called "just in time" ministry. You give people what they need at that moment. You restrain yourself from telling them everything you think they need to know about Jesus, the bible, and salvation. Instead, you notice, respond, care, and connect. There is no need to artificially impose or force-feed spiritual development. There is no need to steer the conversation toward something that has no context in that moment. Restraint is the highest form of discipline among the most highly skilled artists. Jesus was painting on the canvas of this woman's heart. He anticipated that she would be doing most of the preaching to herself.

> When Jesus entered the ruler's house...he said,..."The girl is
> not dead." (Matthew 9:23-24)

When you are on a mission to the missing, conversion and disciple making often get blurred, overlapping and combined like ingredients poured into a mixing bowl. That's why Jesus told us to make disciples, not converts. Conversion is an important but small step toward discipleship. The linear, multistep sequence we think of as a normal path to conversion doesn't happen in reality, even when we have a willing disciplee. There are always twists and turns. Always surprises. If you are too scripted with your evangelistic expectations, you won't be agile enough to stay connected with the people Jesus misses most.

The religious ruler had a tiny mustard-seed faith, but Jesus wanted him to have more, to become more. So on the way to his conversion, Jesus began taking the ruler through "Jesus Following 101." Jesus's "official" disciples were having their own learning experience by watching Jesus make the ruler wait. Then both the ruler and the disciples were baptized into a graduate course in Jesus-followership by practicing restraint as they waited while Jesus helped a woman. And remember, culturally speaking she was the least important type of person Jesus could have spent his valuable time with. The disciples must have wondered: *At least the ruler could influence his followers and help turn this thing into a movement. But a bleeding woman? Please!*

Without saying a word, Jesus was taking them all to school.

When we allow people to belong before they believe, when we include them in the life of our faith community and introduce them to people they would normally never associate with, we are discipling them. Or perhaps more accurately, we're providing a context for them to engage with the Holy Spirit as he teaches them all the truth they need to know at that time.

WJDD

As we consider Jesus's approach to evangelism, think about WJDD— what Jesus *didn't* do. He *didn't*...

- ask the religious ruler, "Why should I help you?"
- seek assurance that the ruler would become his follower.

- explain his rationale to his disciples, who were probably becoming more and more confused.
- worry about how his actions would be perceived by others.
- tell the woman she had to make an appointment so he could work her into his busy schedule.

Jesus made his own rules for evangelism, and look what happened as a result.

ATTEMPTING THE ORDINARY

Even though the biggest part of our day-to-day lives could be described as mundane and repetitive, as Christians we've somehow become addicted to drama and are allergic to the ordinary. We need to embrace the ordinary—which does not mean that our lives have to be boring. It's all about what we see and what we have.

Often, what we have is small—a little time and a little energy. (Remember Jesus's cup-of-cold-water analogy.) So how are we to respond to the people around us, the people whose needs keep cropping up like weeds through the sidewalk? We see them and sense their needs but feel as if we don't have much to give.

We need to realize that much can be done with very little. Here are three really short examples of how someone began to notice what was already going on around her and then chose to give what she had:

- "When I see folks at the grocery store or the post office or on the street, I'm now much more open to looking them in the eye and asking how they're doing. I might even coo at their baby—and I'm not really into cooing at babies!"
- "I finally met the neighbor I've only waved at for two years. I actually introduced myself."
- "Now I stop to talk and listen to another neighbor, an older man with few teeth, when he's out with his dog. I think he doesn't get too many people to listen to him, and he loves to talk."

We need to lose our fascination with drama. Once we give ourselves permission to *not* do something dramatic, we begin to see the
people who have been there all the time.

Everything that is important is already happening around you.
Just begin to notice the missing people who are already part of your
normal social landscape and begin paying attention to them.

CHAPTER 12

A.K.A. "FOUND"

Conversion by Conversation

A fter reading the first eleven chapters of this book, you might wonder what I believe about conversion or coming to faith, or what some refer to as "getting saved." In this book we have focused most of our attention on the *very front end* of the conversion or disciple-making process because that's where most of us ordinary types struggle. When it comes to helping people connect with Jesus, we simply aren't sure how to get started.

Some experts say that it takes about two years for people to move from seeker to finder, from being the missed to seeking the missed. It's a gradual process, not an isolated event. Here are two stories that illustrate how people come to know Jesus as a result of ordinary acts of kindness, free attention giveaways, and Christians doing what is doable.

Spiritual Friendshiping

They couldn't have been more different. Leigh was a veteran Christian, and Diane a committed New Ager. They worked together, and eventually the steamroller known as "life" caught up with Diane, prompting her to ask Leigh some questions.

Diane was "hiring" Leigh to be her spiritual consultant. They were about to develop a spiritual friendship. You may already have someone in your life who has "hired" you to be his spiritual advisor. Here's how you can tell: The person comes up to you and says something like, "Hey, did you see that TV preacher the other night? What was *that* all about?" Or he asks, "Did you read what Jerry Falwell said in the paper?" Or he might say, "Wasn't it cool that the Dalai Lama came to town?"

For some reason that person has decided to trust you. Maybe it's because you don't swear—or maybe it's because you do. Maybe you once let slip a comment about God or Jesus that was authentic and not arrogant, and that person overheard you. Maybe he has been watching you for years and finally decided he would take the risk of revealing a personal struggle. Or perhaps he's so lonely he just forgot that you were a Christian and decided to take a chance on you. Whatever the reason, he's offering you a job as his spiritual advisor.

Here is how Diane and Leigh describe the way their spiritual friendship developed.

Leigh: I've worked at the office I'm in for about nine years.
In an office setting I have always been pretty quiet regarding my faith. When people find out you're a Christian, it has a tendency to shut them down. They begin to watch everything they say in your

presence, they refuse to be themselves, and they
sometimes hold you to a different standard from
others. This doesn't allow me to be myself, since their
version of what I should be like as a Christian may
vary from my own. Eventually, I believe Diane discovered I was a Christian and acknowledged it in
some general conversation. But it continued as a
nonissue, basically.

Then Diane's mother became quite ill with can-
cer, and they weren't sure she would live through the
treatment. I don't know if I said I'd pray for her, but
I may have. Then one day Diane came into the office
and sought me out, saying, "Please pray for my
mom." Or she might have said, "Put in a good word
to the Man up there" or "to the Big Guy." But there
was a real earnestness in her request.

One more thing happened that significantly
changed our conversations about God. We part-
nered on a business program. The scope of this
program required frequent meetings regarding our
business. Business questions gave way to philosophical questions, which gave way to more questions
regarding God.

Diane: I really did not know about Leigh's Christianity until
we started engaging in conversations of greater depth.
Once spirituality became a topic, I became more and
more aware of her "religious base." Because I had
already formed a friendship with Leigh and she had
never approached me with the Jesus talk before, I

never compartmentalized her as a born-again type.
So it didn't occur to me that I should be anticipating
"the talk." Our discussions seemed open and frank
and remarkably free of the canned answers that I had
so often received to my questions.

Leigh's genuine interest in honestly answering my
questions and the fact that she did not discount my
spirituality in order to elevate her position, coupled
with her apparent love of Jesus and God, allowed me
to open up and be receptive to what she was saying.
Our friendship allowed the trust.

Leigh: Diane would ask a philosophical question, and I
would ask right back. This general sharing escalated
into an intense dialogue back and forth. Eventually, it
had to spill into e-mail, to save time and to clarify.
The intensity of her questions just kept increasing.
Also, I remember something significant that doesn't
usually happen with me: The Lord seemed to give
me a picture of Diane's "journey," and I shared it
with her using some of the same language she has
used regarding her spiritual journey. Jesus and I were
able to get her attention by talking about the area of
spiritual gifts. I continued using pictures and themes
and stories almost exclusively in our discussions. I
stayed away from academic types of discussions—
which she was more than capable of diverting into
philosophical discussions. The picture thing worked
really well with her—and I was having a blast coming up with things!

Diane: Ultimately, it all seemed very real, more real than
anything else I had investigated before. With a few
well-timed demonstrations of the aforementioned
"spiritual gifts," it became clearly more than just a
theory to me. It became very tangible and very real.
Most of all it intuitively spoke to me; it made sense.
It was like the pieces of a jigsaw puzzle all locking
into place to form a picture. I began to trust that
what Leigh had to say about Jesus was the truth,
and therefore I knew I had to follow.

When Leigh spoke the good news, it was as a servant. She waited
and watched for signals from Diane. She served the good news before
she shared the good news. She served the gospel by being real, staying
flexible, and using language Diane could understand—the language
of parables and God's power. Diane was intrigued to meet a Christian
who was so real, natural, and kind. She was pleasantly surprised and
overwhelmed by the possibility of a God who might like her, a God
who knew the details of her life. She said yes to Jesus and today leads
a group for women who are spiritual seekers just as she once was.

GO ASK ALICE

In his must-read book *More Ready Than You Realize,* Brian McLaren
introduces us to Alice, a young musician he met at one of his book
signings. Alice is actually April Stace Vega. She and Brian exchanged
e-mails for about a year and a half before she realized that she had
become a follower of Jesus.

As April describes the things that drew her to Jesus, she does not
use the terminology Christians usually associate with conversion stories.

New believers, especially those who have had little contact with the
church, describe their experience with God by using everyday language rather than "Christian" words. For instance, after April became
an acknowledged follower of Jesus, she was still not ready to use the
word *Christian* to describe herself. You can read the full story in
Brian's book, but as a summary, here are some excerpts from an interview I did with Brian and April at an Off The Map event:

> *Jim:* April, after you read one of Brian's earlier books, the
> two of you began an e-mail dialogue. How did that
> impact you spiritually?

> *April:* When he responded to my first e-mail, I was ex-
> tremely surprised. I was surprised that a random pas-
> tor would take a psycho e-mail girl seriously and that
> I, psycho e-mail girl, would take a pastor seriously.
>
> The dialogue with Brian was addictively interest-
> ing. [It] made me question so much about myself,
> my surroundings, and my preconceptions. It's also
> really, really hard not to like it when someone is
> willing to listen to you. I didn't feel that at the time,
> but now that I look back, it was so awesome to be
> able to have an honest conversation with someone
> "knowledgeable."
>
> I never felt like any of his replies were pat or for-
> mulated responses that he used for everyone who had
> the same questions. His replies were personal and
> thoughtful. Honestly, who can not want to be part of
> a conversation like that?

> *Jim:* At what point did you think you might be in the
> process of becoming a Christian?

April: The night of the book signing, I remember feeling overcome and deeply interested. But as far as there being a "crossover point," there was none.

Jim: So you had an experience with God? Were you making a decision?

April: No, not a decision. I just felt deeply touched by deep goodness.

Jim: Brian, when did you think that April might be "coming into the kingdom"?

Brian: I received an e-mail in which she told me about a dream she had about being baptized. I remember thinking that maybe God was trying to tell her something, and she is trying to tell herself something as well. In hindsight I think of that as a significant moment in her journey with Christ.

Jim: Brian, April has said there was no "crossover point" for her. Can you talk some about the crossover concept of conversion?

Brian: I have become more focused on helping everyone (including myself) become better disciples regardless of where they are in the conversion process. For April, reading my book and e-mailing me was part of her becoming a disciple. This [crossover] language of conversion creates an insider/outsider scenario that has a line that places people on one side or the other. There is some validity to that, but it isn't the most interesting way to think about it. For example, we could ask everyone in this room: "What kind of life are you experiencing? Are you really alive?" I think

that's what Jesus meant with his talk about experiencing "life to the full."

Jim: April, how would you describe your conversion: Are
you saved, born again, or converted?

April: None of those labels works for me. I guess I could say
I'm converted in that I attend church and actively try
to follow the way of Christ. I am uncomfortable with
being called "Christian" since I'm unsure of exactly
what it means. It is such a loaded word in our culture.

Do you see some of the currents at work here? All Brian did was
notice April one night when he did a book signing. Then, over time,
he responded to her questions and asked some of his own. It is what
Brian *didn't* do that displays his greatest insight. Like Leigh in the
earlier story, he refused to get in the way of Jesus discipling April by
insisting on advancing his own evangelism agenda.

Is April saved? She says there has been no line for her to cross. Yet
she reports a significant encounter with God that motivated her to ask
more questions. People begin drawing closer to Jesus long before there
is an identifiable point of "conversion." Modern-day evangelicalism
has attempted to remove the mystery and wonder from the conversion process. It has attempted to reduce it to a transaction. But birth
is always messy.

Today April is studying for her Master of Divinity and serves in a
local church as director of arts and worship. Her husband is youth
pastor at Brian McLaren's church in Maryland.

I am one of those people who know the exact date, place, and
time of day I decided to pray the prayer to accept Jesus as my personal
Lord and Savior. A specific crossover point for conversion worked for
me. So why don't I talk about that?

Here's why:

Americans feel tremendous freedom to construct their own
religious perspectives and practices, regardless of traditions and
time-honored teachings. It is amazing that we live in a period
during which people are more interested in spirituality than at
any time in the past half century, yet they are seeking answers
to their spiritual questions and needs from sources other than
Christian churches. The American public is sending a clear
message to Christian leaders: Make Christianity accessible and
practical or don't expect their participation.[1]

Simply put, things have changed. In the terminology of war, it
would be described as the situation on the ground becoming "fluid."
Just because something worked in the past doesn't make it sacred now.
The mission matters more than the method. Nothing is sacred except
Jesus, *full stop.*

We've shrunk our understanding of what it means to follow Jesus
down to a four-point contract that today's spiritual seekers aren't buying. We need to adapt to the spiritual realities of our environment.

Southwest Airlines adapted.

The deer tick adapted.

John Harrison, inventor of the chronometer, adapted.

Jesus adapted.

Will we adapt?

ORDINARY ATTEMPTS PRACTICE GUIDE

Ordinary Attempts are practices any of us can do without prior training or special expertise. They are relational acts of kindness, *free attention giveaways*. They include things such as the following:

- Asking someone "how are you?"—and then actually listening.
- Praying for people "behind their backs" and telling them later.
- Asking a tip-sensitive server in a restaurant about his or her life outside of work.
- Listening to someone. (Do this to almost anyone, and that person will think you're really cool.)
- Giving away a little money.

Why Practice Ordinary Attempts?

Jesus made it clear that Ordinary Attempts count, even when we think they don't. He said, "If you give a cup of cold water to a little child because you are my disciple you won't lose your reward" (Matthew 10:42, author's paraphrase). Our culture's equivalent of a cup of cold water is *attention*. Ordinary Attempts involve giving away our attention for free, which helps us connect with the people Jesus misses most.

What Values Inform Ordinary Attempts?

Not only is this practice ordinary, it's also simple. Ordinary Attempts are based on such values as the following:
- *Think small.* Don't change the world, just change *something*.
- *Say "wow."* Make a big deal out of small stuff.
- *Do what's doable.* It's all you're going to do anyway.
- *Count what matters.* Conversations, not conversions.
- *Be yourself.* It will intrigue people.

Why a Practice Guide?

Programs can be helpful, but they often fail in the long run because, like diets, they're someone else's idea. What we need are *practices*— simple, memorable activities that can be done by ordinary people as part of their *normal routine*. No special training necessary. No unusual courage required.

The practices in this book will help you "angle into" the life of a missing person. Some practices are overt, and some aren't even detectable. Each can be tailored to fit the situation and the person you are attempting to connect with. The basic rule is to be real, not religious. In the same way that pushy salespeople turn us off, religious people turn off missing people. And believe me, they see us coming. So keep it real!

We learn by doing, not simply discussing. In most of life the word *training* means "hands on"—think golf, cooking, computers, swimming, or piano. Unfortunately, in the church the idea of training too often means attending a class.

Ordinary Attempts can be done by individuals or groups, but I encourage you to meet with a few other Christians. Team up with a friend or with your small group, youth group, prayer group, bible-study group, Sunday-school class, or men's or women's group. Decide to do something ordinary to start connecting with the people Jesus misses most; then give it a try. Afterward, get together with others so that all of you can tell your stories and share observations.

As you seek to connect with the people formerly known as "lost," use the practical suggestions provided at the end of each of the first eleven chapters in the section called Attempting the Ordinary.

For a free downloadable copy of an Ordinary Attempts study guide, go to www.off-the-map.org/oa. You can also purchase preprinted guides at www.off-the-map.org/store.

PAY SOMEONE TO CRITIQUE YOUR CHURCH

H ere's a great way to help yourself and your congregation (or small group) gain a more complete understanding of what the people formerly known as "lost" think of Christians and the church. You simply pay them for their opinion. There is no better way to gauge how we come across to those God misses most than to ask them.

If you really want to make a connection with a missing person, give this a try. Hire a missing person to critique your church, your bible-study group, or your spiritual-support group. People will gladly tell you their opinion of how Christians come across to them as long as you take them seriously and don't use this as a ploy to "preach" to them.

Getting Started

Photocopy the survey on pages 149-152, or go to *www.off-the-map* *.org/oa*, and download the church survey. Feel free to make as many copies as you like.

Tell your missing friend that all he or she has to do is attend a weekend service (or a meeting of your small group or other Christian gathering) and then fill out the survey. It will take about an hour, and the person will receive twenty-five dollars for doing the survey.

For your own information, the survey questions are designed to do the following:

- Make the missing person feel in control.
- Provide you with valuable insights as to how your church (or small group) is experienced by the people we say we are primarily trying to reach.
- Create an on-ramp for you into the life of a person who might be willing to keep the conversation going.
- Send a message to the people in your church or small group that connecting with the people Jesus misses most is not only doable but fun.

Survey Tips

Handpick the missing person you want to participate in this survey. Find someone you or someone else in your group has a relationship with. It could be a waitress, a bartender, a barista, a schoolmate, or a co-worker. Then have some fun when you issue the invitation. I often open with something like this:

Hey, Debbie. I'm involved with a group of people who are trying to figure out why folks don't like church and why they tend to avoid Christians. We're tired of discussing it among ourselves, so we decided to get feedback from some people we like who don't regularly attend church. I was wondering if you'd be willing to do a survey for me. By the way, do you go to church regularly? [In this context, *regularly* means about once a month. If they say they do attend that often, ask where and say, "Wow, great!" Thank them and ask if they know someone who doesn't attend church. About 90 percent of the time, the first person you approach will meet the requirement.]

You don't attend regularly? Okay. I'd like you to come to our church (or bible-study group or spiritual-support group) one time and tell us what your experience there is like. You'll have to attend a church service (or a group meeting) and fill out a survey. It'll take about an hour, *but* you don't have to participate or anything. All we ask is that you observe what's going on and then answer several written questions. We'll pay you twenty-five dollars for your help! Your insights are valuable to us, so it's worth it.

If the person says he doesn't care about the money, just say, "No, we really feel better about this if we can pay for your time." If he continues to push it, tell him, "We'll work it out." (I've never had a person refuse the money or a twenty-five dollar gift certificate on site.)

Assure him that this isn't a bait-and-switch deal in which someone will call or visit his home afterward without his permission. Tell him that you'll sit with him during the service (or meeting) to answer any questions or explain anything he may be wondering about.

It's important that he feel you really want the information and aren't just setting him up. Be sure that you personally meet him at church and sit with him. Give him the survey at church, not before. Don't draw attention to him—"Hey, this is the guy we've hired to do that survey from a non-Christian's perspective!"

When the service (or meeting) is over, take his filled-out survey and give him a handwritten thank-you card with cash or a gift card inside. (Don't give him a check. Instant gratification is better!) Tell the person you'll touch base with him later that week—wherever you normally see the person. Then send the person on his way. You will pleasantly surprise the person by not pressuring him in any way.

Follow-Up

Read the survey responses and glean one or two insights. Share those insights with your church or small group. Ask fellow church members (or group members) to ask other missing persons if that information fits their perceptions as well.

Check back with your survey buddy about a week later to ask him or her about any "after" feelings. Stay connected with the person and use this experience as an on-ramp into his or her life.

SURVEY

Thanks for taking time to help us. We've asked you to give us your feedback because you don't attend our church regularly. While we appreciate positive feedback, we are primarily looking for constructive criticism. We want to see our church through your eyes. Please answer the following questions:

1. What were your very first impressions—how did you feel coming into "our space"? Nothing is too trivial to mention.

2. What is the name of the first person who introduced him- or herself to you today? Did you know this person before you came here?

3. Was the building easy to find? How about our signs? What would you do differently?

4. As you sit and observe us, do we seem sincere? forced? fake? Why?

5. What do you think about our rituals (we call it a liturgy or a program)?

6. Are you able to understand why we do what we do? What do you think we're trying to do with our approach to "doing church."

7. If applicable, write down the feelings you had watching people sing.

8. What was the speaker trying to get across in his or her talk?

9. On a scale of one to ten, with ten meaning "off the charts" and one meaning "boring," how would you rank the following:
    Singing _____
    Preaching or speaking _____
    Prayer and Scripture reading _____
    Reciting creeds or other material in unison _____

Please explain your rankings:

10. What do you think we're trying to accomplish in this meeting?

11. Check out our church program/bulletin. If the program asks visitors to give their name and other information, how did you feel about that request?

12. If you were in charge of running this church, what are three things you would change right away? (Please be candid.)

   1.

   2.

   3.

13. Tell us anything else we may have forgotten to ask about, but you think would be good for us to think about.

14. Would you be willing to provide the following information
    so we can check back with you to ask if you have any
    other thoughts or impressions about your experience?
    Name _____
    Phone _____
    Address _____
    City _____ Zip _____
    E-mail _____

15. May we call you if we have follow-up questions regarding
    your responses?
    [ ] Yes
    [ ] No

NOTES

Chapter 1

1. Joseph L. Badaracco Jr., *Leading Quietly: An Unorthodox Guide to Doing the Right Thing* (Boston: Harvard Business School Press, 2002), 1. Emphasis added.

Chapter 2

1. Jessica Stern, *Terror in the Name of God: Why Religious Militants Kill* (New York: HarperCollins, 2003), 28.

Chapter 3

1. See Stephen Ambrose, *D Day, June 6, 1944: The Climactic Battle of World War II* (New York: Touchstone, 1995), 357.
2. Darin Erstad, quoted in Larry Stone, "Erstad Preceded Ichiro in Hit Chase," *Seattle Times,* September 14, 2004, http://seattle times.nwsource.com/text/2002034628_mariside14.html.

Chapter 4

1. For more on the invention of the chronometer and its far-reaching impact, see Dava Sobel, *Longitude: The True Story of a Lone Genius Who Solved the Greatest Scientific Problem of His Time* (New York: Walker & Company, 1995).
2. Arno Karlen, *Biography of a Germ* (New York: Pantheon, 2000), 93.

3. Adapted from Rachelle Mee-Chapman, "Picking Up Trash for Jesus," *Idealab,* October 2004, www.off-the-map.org/idealab/04-10/trash.html. Rachelle Chapman pastors ThPM (www.thursdaypm.org), a missional community in Seattle, Washington. She also contributes stories regularly to Off The Map.

Chapter 5

1. For more on these ideas, see John Locke, *The De-Voicing of Society: Why We Don't Talk to Each Other Anymore* (New York: Simon & Schuster, 1998), 18, 28, 39, 61.

2. Locke, *The De-Voicing of Society,* 61.

3. George G. Hunter, *The Celtic Way of Evangelism: How Christianity Can Reach the West…Again* (Nashville: Abingdon, 2000), 99. Emphasis added.

4. Hunter, *The Celtic Way,* 21.

5. Hunter, *The Celtic Way,* 77. Emphasis added.

6. Hunter, *The Celtic Way,* 32.

7. Dana Colwell, quoted in Associated Press "Bra Saves Woman's Life," *Detroit News,* June 11, 2001, www.detnews.com/2001/metro/0106/10/metro-234106.htm.

8. Hunter, *The Celtic Way,* 89.

9. Conrad H. Gempf, *Jesus Asked: What He Wanted to Know* (Grand Rapids: Zondervan, 2003), 13.

Chapter 6

1. Conrad H. Gempf, *Jesus Asked: What He Wanted to Know* (Grand Rapids: Zondervan, 2003), 144.

Chapter 7

1. Quoted from a private conversation with Dr. Dan B. Allender, September 2000.

2. The 10 percent rule had an even more dramatic impact during World War II. The military needed a small landing craft that "could pass over floating logs and sandbars without damaging the rudder." Andrew Jackson Higgins, builder of the Higgins boat (which General Dwight D. Eisenhower credited with winning the war), had "seen a film in which blue whales, the largest mammals in the world, had displayed great maneuverability and speed." His builders began "experimenting with bow designs that would incorporate the lines of the whales' jaw and forward belly. The first experiment led to an increase in the boats' speed of almost ten percent." (Jerry E. Strahan, *Andrew Jackson Higgins and the Boats That Won World War II* (Baton Rouge: Louisiana State University Press, 1994), 16-17.

3. The story is attributed to James Graeser Jr., "Taboo" (sermon, Cross+Road Lutheran, Orange Park, FL, April 6, 2003). Historical veracity could not be determined.

Chapter 8

1. Adapted from "Uncommon Friends," the video account of the friendship between John Barce and the young gay student, www.off-the-map.org/mediacenter.

2. Herb Kelleher, quoted in Kevin Freiberg and Jackie Freiberg, *Nuts: Southwest Airlines' Crazy Recipe for Business and Personal Success* (Austin, TX: Bard Press, 1996), 54.

Chapter 9

1. Benson Bobrick, *Angel in the Whirlwind: The Triumph of the American Revolution* (New York: Penguin, 1998), 429.

2. Steve Sjogren is one of the most innovative evangelism entrepreneurs of our time. The church he planted, The Vineyard Community Church in Cincinnati (www.cincyvineyard.com), commits a significant percentage of its income to researching creative ways to connect with people using a unique approach called Servant Evangelism. You can find out more about Steve's work at www.servantevangelism.com.

Chapter 10

1. Charles Seife, *Zero: The Biography of a Dangerous Idea* (New York: Penguin, 2000), 39.

2. Seife, *Zero,* 5.

Chapter 11

1. This story is used by permission of Richard Bott, St. Marys United Church, St. Marys, Ontario, Canada, http://richard.peacefulwaters.org.

Chapter 12

1. George Barna, quoted in Marv Knox, "Ranks of 'Unchurched' Growing, Barna Says," *Biblical Recorder,* March 19, 1999, www.biblicalrecorder.com/news/3_19_99/ranks.html.

ABOUT THE AUTHOR

JIM HENDERSON has been involved in church planting and leadership development for the past twenty-five years. He has worked with young leaders and church plants in the United States, India, and Hong Kong. Jim formerly worked at the Vineyard Community Church (known for leading the Servant Evangelism movement) in Cincinnati, Ohio, as director of leadership development and director of outreach.

Jim is an innovative thinker who in 2000 cofounded Off The Map to help reinvent evangelism for ordinary Christians. Off The Map holds numerous events each year and publishes free content on its Web site as well as a free monthly e-zine titled *Idealab*. Jim and his wife, Barb, have three children and live in Seattle.

For more information about *a.k.a. "Lost,"* Ordinary Attempts, reinventing evangelism, or Off The Map, visit *www.off-the-map.org* or *www.akalost.com,* or contact Jim Henderson at *jim@off-the-map.org.*

What do *lost* people think?

The *Lost* Interviews
Those who aren't born again talk back to those who are

akalost.com
[free video]